Praise for
Growing Up at Work

"This is a deeply insightful and practical book. It brings individuals to life right before your eyes. Yael Sivi and Yosh Beier are great storytellers and clear explicators—you'll welcome their voice."

—**BOB KAPLAN,** PhD, author of *The Versatile Leader: Make the Most of Your Strengths Without Overdoing It*

"*Growing Up At Work* beautifully brings complex theory into practice. Through their engaging, detailed client stories, Sivi and Beier elegantly convey how Adult Development Theory and Gestalt come to life in their work with clients. I believe that professionals, leaders, and coaches will all benefit from this book and the wisdom and experience it offers."

—**LISA LASKOW LAHEY,** Ed.D, author, Harvard School of Education faculty, co-author of *Immunity to Change: How to Overcome It and Unlock the Potential in Yourself and Your Organization*

"A truly revolutionary book, transforming how we see personal and professional growth in the workplace. *Growing Up at Work*'s riveting stories are the ultimate guide to becoming more emotionally and socially mature, both at work and at home."

—**MARSHALL GOLDSMITH,** the *New York Times* No. 1 bestselling author of *Triggers, Mojo,* and *What Got You Here Won't Get You There*

"*Growing Up At Work* took me on an adventure of learning about myself, my leadership, and how the two are inextricably interconnected. Sivi and Beier unpack complex concepts and provide concrete ways to get to the crux of problems in our work and in our lives. This book explores the cognitive dissonance of knowing that we are grownups yet continually finding ourselves in situations where we feel thrown off balance. The authors take this human dilemma and forge a pathway for us to find our centers through vibrant, deeply human stories in which you are guaranteed to see yourself and others. A *tour de force*."

—ROBERT BANK, president and CEO,
American Jewish World Service

"*Growing Up at Work* is an important, unique, and moving account of the journeys of these many people to do exactly what the title says: grow up at work. This book will touch the reader and also give hope to any who struggle in the world of work. It is unusual because it combines the theory of Gestalt psychotherapy with its more universal application outside of the therapy room. Make no mistake, though; this book inspires the work of change, discovery, and courage."

—JOHANNA BARRETT, LCSW, ACSW,
faculty at Gestalt Associates for Psychotherapy

"This book is truly inspired and inspiring. Yael and Yosh bring a wealth of compassionate and practical wisdom to bear on a range of specific dilemmas faced by those wishing to embody more skillful leadership. Creatively combining psychological understanding along with decades of organizational experience, they offer profound guidance on what it means to heal and to grow, not just as leaders but as human beings—and not just at the workplace but in all of one's life."

—LAURA O'LOUGHLIN, LCSW, co-founder
and Dharma teacher, Brooklyn Zen Center

"This book offers the much-needed reminder that our private and public lives are not separate; indeed, how we navigate our inner worlds is how we show up at work. Yael and Yosh, through clear and relatable story-telling, show us that to be effective at work, we must 'do the work,' that is to bring the unconscious to the conscious for healing and growth. As someone who has not only benefited from the wisdom in this book, but has been personally coached by them, I can assure readers that Yael and Yosh's practical and reflective tools will lead to both greater personal and business success."

—KERRY DOCHERTY, cofounder
and chief impact officer, Faherty Brand

"I have seen firsthand how Yael's insights and experiences have signifi-cantly impacted the over 120 participants she has taught in the Emerging Leaders program of Princeton AlumniCorps. As the lead facilitator, she has fostered a space for authentic and experiential learning and trans-formation. I'm thrilled that this book will provide her perceptive and actionable advice to a broader audience. Millennials have experienced many national and global traumas in their formative years and are now 'growing up at work' in an environment no one could have anticipated. This book will be invaluable to all leaders in this challenging and uncer-tain time."

—KEF KASDIN, board president and
former executive director, Princeton AlumniCorps

"*Growing Up at Work* is a must-read for anyone in a leadership posi-tion. As someone who has personally been coached by Yael Sivi, I have experienced firsthand how the teachings in this book open the door to stronger and more emotionally intelligent leadership."

—SARAH LARSON LEVEY, founder/CEO, Y-7 Studio

"I thoroughly enjoyed this book. Sivi and Beier engage us immediately with their ability to take complex concepts and make them digestible. They take us on an easy-to-follow journey as they weave practice, theory, and coaching narratives together. The writing is skillful and without jargon."

—**JOSEPH MELNICK,** founding editor of *Gestalt Review* and
co-author of *The Evolution of the Cape Cod Model:
Gestalt Conversations, Theory and Practice*

Growing Up at Work

HOW TO **TRANSFORM** PERSONALLY,
EVOLVE PROFESSIONALLY,
AND **LEAD AUTHENTICALLY**

Yael C. Sivi
and Yosh C. Beier

RIVER GROVE
BOOKS

Published by River Grove Books
Austin, TX
www.rivergrovebooks.com

Distributed by River Grove Books

Design and composition by Greenleaf Book Group
Cover design by Greenleaf Book Group and Mimi Bark

Publisher's Cataloging-in-Publication data is available.

Print ISBN: 978-1-63299-374-8

eBook ISBN: 978-1-63299-375-5

First Edition

For Noah, our beloved companion, our little guy, the bacon between the bread. Thank you for your understanding, flexibility, and humor as we wrote this book. We hope that reading it will one day help you understand our work even more deeply.

And to our parents, Isak, Marti, Karl-Heinz, and Christa, for supporting and loving us always.

Contents

Preface

SIGMUND FREUD BELIEVED THAT THERE were two primary hall-marks of adulthood: *to love and to work.*

Ask most adults what brings them joy, and these two things are likely to be at the top of their list. For nearly two decades, we've coached dozens of organizational leaders and teams, and we're more convinced than ever that work is one of the most significant markers of adulthood—an experience full of meaning and rich in opportunities for growth.

In fact, love and work for us are indelibly intertwined. We met in 2003 at the Esalen Institute in California's Big Sur. We fell in love while doing dishes, chopping strawberries, and preparing meals in the kitchen as part of Esalen's work-scholar program. When we took breaks, we didn't really take breaks. Instead, we sat outside with our coworkers and processed the interpersonal dynamics of working together. Taking part in these sessions in the middle of the workday felt revolutionary, edgy, and enlivening to us.

What became clear to us is that the workplace (in person or remote) is not just somewhere to get work done, but it's also a laboratory for personal and interpersonal growth. We discovered that everything that seemed work-related on the surface had deeper emotional or psychological origins. Micromanagement was often a sign of control issues that needed attention. Strained relationships became openings to develop greater empathy and emotional honesty with others. Overwork could be addressed by setting healthier boundaries. As a result, individuals evolved, and relationships blossomed.

Work, it turns out, gives us the opportunities not only to be more effective and collaborative but also to truly understand ourselves. Work gives us the chance to *grow up*.

Fast forward to 2010, when we cofounded Collaborative Coaching, a New York-based executive coaching and consulting firm.

Yael, who is also a licensed Gestalt psychotherapist, has helped clients ranging from American Express and Coca-Cola to the United Nations and US Forest Service. As an executive coach and organizational consultant, her expertise is helping leaders and teams grow by supporting interpersonal dynamics and emotional maturity at work. Trained as a scientist, consultant, mediator, and therapist, Yosh speaks the language of human and organizational dynamics. He holds a Master of Science in theoretical physics from the Technical University Berlin and a professional degree in strategic-decision and risk management from Stanford University, and is licensed as a psychotherapist and mediator.

Esalen still feels close to our consciousness. In fact, the tagline for our company takes its inspiration from our experience there: *Authentic Interactions. Extraordinary Results.* The institute is where the founder of Gestalt therapy, Fritz Perls, spent the end of his life, and the ethos and language of this form of psychotherapy continues to deeply inform us professionally and personally—as a married couple with a young child—in two important ways.

On one level, we recognize and unravel reliable, predictable, and common professional challenges faced by many people at work, especially in leadership. Issues such as imposter syndrome, navigating power dynamics, dealing with feelings of inadequacy, or suffering from a lack of work-life balance are commonplace and require our attention.

But on a deeper level, we understand that what may often look like workplace challenges are actually more personal in nature. (Consider the Esalen kitchen). To mature professionally, we must be willing to *grow up* emotionally and psychologically, too. The stories in this book will show you how it's possible to do that—to make the unconscious conscious and more closely examine and transform the ways in which you live and work in the world.

In our experience, the very best leaders transcend personal limitations so they can act with maturity, self-awareness, honesty, dependability, and kindness. We believe that emotionally mature leaders create healthy employees, teams, and organizations—and by extension, enhance their influence. Professional growth and personal growth are intertwined, and authentic, positive, lasting leadership growth requires self-awareness and openness to deep personal growth—in other words, *growth from the inside out*. While there is no quick fix, our experience has shown that extraordinary results are possible.

We wrote this book to share our lessons and insights about our coaching work with you. Our hope is that you can see yourself in one or more of the stories and get a clearer understanding of the emotional and psychological terrain that might lie underneath your professional landscape, and how to work through it in healthy and productive ways.

A couple of things to note: Because we work so closely together and provide each other with peer supervision related to our coaching, this book serves as a reflection of our collaboration over many years. You'll notice that the prologue, introduction, and conclusion are written in the "we" voice. However, because the following eleven stories are based on Yael's coaching work with clients, the "I" in each story is Yael.

It's also worth mentioning that we wrote most of this book when we all still thought of work as *a place* we went. In the wake of the

COVID-19 pandemic, however, the shift from work *as a place we go* to *a thing we do* has accelerated. We continue to coach clients, but for now, all of our work is online.

While it's doubtful that the workplace as we know it will ever be the same, professional and leadership challenges remain. So do the emotional and psychological issues that require our care and attention to be transformed. We believe our book is just as relevant now as it was pre-pandemic, even as the existential ground beneath our feet shifts.

We think you'll agree, too, that it's never too late to grow up and see yourself, and others, more deeply and authentically in everything you do.

Introduction

Lifelong Practices for Personal Transformation and Professional Evolution

IN ALL OF OUR WORK, we are constantly reminded that changing behavior on the surface, while sometimes effective, is often not sustainable. It's our belief and experience that the deepest and most meaningful change comes *from the inside out*.

When we closely examine and shift our behaviors and patterns, transformation is possible. For transformation to occur, we must grow *and* change. This takes time—and sustained practice. Using in-depth client stories as a way to illustrate what integrated personal and professional growth looks like, we portray this process realistically and in ways that we hope will encourage you to do your own work.

In this book, you'll find the following:

1. **Lifelong practices for personal transformation and professional evolution** that we introduce to clients and that you can bring into your own life.

2. **Theories and concepts** underpinning our coaching approach, which centers around Gestalt therapy, a humanistic form of psychotherapy grounded in the present moment experience of the client and the therapist, as well as Adult Development Theory, a model that describes how our consciousness can evolve in adulthood.

3. **Client stories** based on our real-life coaching and therapy experiences with adults of all ages at different stages in their careers.

The client stories that contain distinguishing personal information have been reviewed and approved by the respective clients. In some cases, we have changed identifying details or created a composite character based on more than one person.

Without exception, the individuals featured in these poignant and inspiring stories realized that how they worked was no longer working for them. These are stories that are usually cloaked in confidentiality and aren't always widely shared. But they reflect us all back to ourselves, since each of us is familiar with the challenges work can pose for our psyche—feeling like an imposter, a tendency to avoid conflict, or an intense desire to be liked, among others.

These clients either sought coaching themselves, or they were sent to us by their organization. For some, these lessons came early in their career. For others, it took decades of professional life for them to realize something needed to shift—or to build the courage and conviction to act on their growing insights.

Each chapter is written around a central and common work dilemma faced by adults, whether they are leaders or not. We'll describe the issue and walk you through our coaching process. Where relevant, the implications for leadership are also discussed since the emotional journeys our clients took had positive effects on their ability to lead. Because all of our clients are high functioning, we consider the work we did with them as essentially a form of "assisted self-discovery," a term used by Ron Kurtz, the founder of Hakomi therapy. This form of therapy, in which Yosh is certified, has deep roots in Gestalt therapy. In this sense, our coaching is slightly unconventional, in that it sits at the intersection of leadership development and Gestalt psychotherapy. As a consequence, we tend to work best with clients who are willing to do more "experiential" work with us based on curiosity, honesty, and depth.

We conclude each chapter by looking at what the client learned and how they applied that knowledge to their personal and professional life. We also offer you opportunities for reflection, experimentation, and concrete practices to try related to the chapter's central dilemma.

Achieving a richer, more meaningful life

All of the client stories in this book begin with a professional challenge, which, upon investigation, reveals itself as a deeper, psychological dilemma inviting transformation. Personal transformation is not simply about acquiring knowledge or skills; it involves foundational shifts in how we perceive ourselves and the world around us. This work will also unlock more authentic, effective leadership—because rather than showing up as someone we believe we should be, we show up as ourselves.

Over time, we've learned that the kind of personal transformation we describe in the client stories is best supported through a general set of lifelong *practices* that transcend specific dilemmas. We use the word *practices* purposefully: The most rewarding and meaningful changes in life aren't the result of a quick fix. Rather, change is the result of daily, intentional, and conscious choices that enable us to shift out of habitual ways of thinking into newer approaches to our lives. In Buddhist teachings, there is a saying: True understanding cannot be separated from action. Insight alone can't bring about transformation—but insight combined with ongoing practice can.

Though the practices we outline build on each other, they appear here in a numbered list for ease of use rather than as a chronological roadmap. Depending on your history, temperament, and dilemma, you may need to focus on a few practices at once, and the practice best suited for you may shift over time.

What follows are thirteen *lifelong practices for personal transformation and professional evolution* that you can use to achieve a richer, more meaningful life.

13 LIFELONG PRACTICES FOR PERSONAL TRANSFORMATION AND PROFESSIONAL EVOLUTION

1. Start where you are
2. Take inventory of the voices in your head
3. Notice when the past is present
4. Take back your eyes
5. Stand up to your inner critic
6. Practice the power of the pause
7. Do something different
8. Create healthy boundaries
9. Develop real empathy for others
10. Speak truth with care
11. Find your own voice
12. Be the adult in the room
13. Be kind to yourself

1. Start where you are

More often than not, our clients begin a coaching session by telling us what they don't want to feel. They say, "I'm scared of managing this new team but what I really want is to feel excitement about it." On the surface, this makes sense, and it's very human not to want to feel—let alone embrace—uncomfortable emotions.

Inherent in our coaching work, however, is something called the "paradoxical theory of change," a concept that rose to prominence in the field through the work of Gestalt therapist Arnold Beisser. As the name of the theory suggests, the only chance we have to change our lives begins with acknowledging, accepting, and experiencing *where we are starting from and how we actually feel*. We must learn to feel our fear if we wish to eventually feel excited. We must acknowledge we are angry before we can forgive. By starting with where we are, we direct our energy to what's actually true instead of resisting what's actually happening (which *takes* energy).

When we acknowledge and feel what we experience, we release energy otherwise bound up in resisting. There's a well-known therapy maxim: "What we resist, persists." By not resisting, we create an opportunity for something new to occur. Only then do we have a chance to actually change.

2. Take inventory of the voices in your head

One of the things that can startle new clients is the realization that they have voices in their head. When we first bring up this idea, some people start worrying they have multiple personalities. But the truth is, all of us have various voices in our head and contrasting ways of looking at ourselves.

These voices represent various aspects of our history, different levels of consciousness, and distinct belief systems. On the inside, we are not all that consistent. We might have an inner voice of fear (who sounds a lot like a child), and we might also have an inner voice of trust (who sounds a lot like a mature adult). We might hear a voice that sounds like our mother's anxiety or another that resembles our father's sense of self-importance.

Learning to navigate these voices starts with simply acknowledging their existence. Sometimes, we call it a "roll call." Name all the voices in your head to discern their perspectives. Then notice if any of those voices sound like one of your parents or family members or simply a harsh version of yourself. Many times, what we seek in our work with clients is to get them to start having a conversation, or dialogue, among their different voices to gain a greater understanding and perspective.

Even though it may take a while, what we're looking to do is to bring into awareness all the things that are out of our awareness but nonetheless influence us. In other words, it's a form of "making the unconscious conscious," a key concept from psychotherapy. For instance, we may *think* we want to be cooperative with colleagues, but when it comes down to it, we are informed by a distrustful inner voice that tells us our colleagues aren't worthy of our cooperation.

Another useful dimension in taking inventory is to practice asking ourselves a question offered by Brené Brown, "What is the story I'm telling myself about this?" By paying attention to our inner narrative, we may come to realize that our negative feelings are almost always the result of our beliefs. We may come to realize that we are actually in conflict with *ourselves*, only once we slow down enough to identify the voices inside.

3. Notice when the past is present

The past is often present in our lives. We often don't realize it, but many of us walk around with emotional issues that remain unresolved from our childhood. This might include a sense of low self-worth, a belief that we need to be liked by everyone, or a perception that we must avoid conflict to be safe.

Negative self-beliefs usually stem from early life experiences, often with important figures like family members, friends, or community members. Until we notice when the past is present and choose something different, we will continue to unconsciously play out the past dramas of our lives with the people around us (in psychoanalysis, this dynamic is known as transference).

When we notice that the past is present, however, we are invited to step back and realize what's *actually* going on for us and how our history might be creeping into the present moment. A question we often like to ask in this respect is, "Does this dynamic remind you of anything from your past?" By mining the past, understanding it, and working to heal it, we have the chance to show up differently.

4. Take back your eyes

Without realizing it, we often perceive ourselves by imagining how other people see us (projection). We see ourselves through *their* eyes instead of our own. Unless we suffer from a chronic sense of grandiosity, most of us tend to imagine that others see us more negatively than they actually do. We feel bad as a result. Taking back our eyes is an ongoing invitation to stop doing this.

In reality, we may never know exactly what another thinks or feels about us, and it can be consuming and deeply distracting to see ourselves through the imagined perceptions of others. Fritz Perls suggested a bold antidote to this end: "What you think of me," he's reported to have said, "is none of my business."

Once we take back our eyes, we come back to our own senses and we return to ourselves. We begin by realizing that if we feel bad, then it's very likely that we are actually *hurting ourselves* through a self-attack in our heads. We're invited to treat ourselves with the love and respect we crave from others, which is its own lifelong practice.

5. Stand up to your inner critic

Amid the cacophony of voices inside us, many have a prominent inner critic in our heads. This is the inner voice that criticizes us—and in some cases, attacks us (retroflection). Some inner critics are so loud and mean that they are better described as inner dictators or bullies. Some never shut up.

While some forms of inner critique or self-control can be useful (e.g., feeling guilty if we hurt someone's feelings), our inner critic often attacks a lot of what we do, and this leads us to feeling bad. We're subject to a litany of inner negativity unknowingly created and received all by ourselves. It's as if we have a critic walking around with us at all times, focusing on all of our perceived mistakes.

Waking up to how much we self-attack, and how it affects us, can transform how we feel. If you suffer from feelings of inadequacy, it is very likely that you actually have an inner critic that is telling you that you're not enough.

Once we become aware of this habit, we must learn to stand up to our inner attacker. We must shore up our confidence and feel love for the other parts of ourselves—especially the part of us that is being bullied. We must learn to defend ourselves and break the bond with our inner attacker.

One of the simplest ways to do this is to practice saying simple things to yourself like "Stop," "Enough," or "I got this." This inner critic, or bully, has pushed many of us for most of our lives, and the first step is to let it know that it isn't in charge anymore. There is a wiser, more mature Self that is stepping in.

(Note: throughout this book, when "Self" is capitalized we are referring to the Self that Carl Jung, Richard Schwartz, and others have discussed as our higher Self—the part of us guided by natural confidence, ease and trust in ourselves and in life. This is in contrast to a smaller sense of "self" dominated by ego needs to be liked, significant, or in control.)

With time, we are also invited to befriend our inner critic, which at first can feel counterintuitive. When clients come to see this side of themselves, many are reluctant to do this part—they are usually more inclined to destroy their inner critic. But because it's a part of us, trying to kill off the inner attacker doesn't work; it creates more division and inner strife. We are invited to spend time getting to know this part of ourselves. We learn why it attacks us to feel safe in the world, and with that understanding, we ask the attacker to help us in new and different ways.

6. Practice the power of the pause

It may sound simple, but it's not easy: We can change a moment with a pause. The power of the pause involves slowing down, especially when we want to speed up. That might mean staying quiet when we would normally raise our voice out of frustration, breathing calmly instead of getting defensive, or taking a minute to consider our options before automatically avoiding a difficult conversation.

Pausing involves bringing our attention to our present-moment experience and deepening our breathing. It also involves sensing the physical sensations in our bodies and waiting a few counts—if not more. We do this so we can help our nervous systems relax, especially if we've been agitated or upset in any way.

We pause so that we can listen to ourselves and not simply react. We pause so that we can tap into our inner voice. We pause so that we can make a *choice* and not simply go on autopilot—or do what we habitually and unconsciously do. As Pema Chödrön, a deeply respected Buddhist teacher, advises, "Don't bite the hook." By that she means don't react to life without contemplation and choice. If you have ever received feedback that you are reactive, then the pause is your friend.

Over time, the practice of pausing adds up. If all we do is pause more consistently, more regularly, and with more awareness, we can make a tremendous difference in our lives. After we coach leaders for several months, one of their most consistent takeaways is the need to practice pausing more regularly.

7. Do something different

Pausing is critical. But if we want to up the ante, once we pause, we grow when we *do something different*. This lesson is about showing up, communicating, leading, or behaving in a new way—for you and your habitual way of being in the world.

If you usually approach difficult conversations with your boss from a place of passivity, practice staying connected to your assertiveness and directness instead and saying the thing that you're scared to say. If you tend to get defensive or face turf battles with your peers, take note of that pattern (notice if your past is present!) and listen to be influenced by others. Notice when your jaw is clenched and try to relax it.

Doing something new can look like many different things, depending on your own specific patterns, the voices in your head, and your history. At the highest level, it's showing up from a mindset of taking responsibility. It's about experimenting with creative and fresh ways of relating to yourself and others.

8. Create healthy boundaries

Some of us have a habitual and chronic way of going along to get along (confluence). We regularly yield to others' wishes and override our own needs on a regular basis to reduce the possibility of differences or disagreement with others. We may not even know our own needs.

Most of us learned to do this early in our lives, often in relation to overbearing relatives or in families or social situations where going along allowed us to feel safe.

In the workplace, we exercise a fair amount of going along every day—and some of it is functional. For instance, we might support an initiative with which we initially disagreed to avoid a lengthy conflict with our team. Or we might avoid a difficult conversation with one of our peers because we don't think the issue is worth it. These actions can serve us and our relationships.

However, when we do this chronically and without self-awareness, going along and deferring our own needs becomes a problem. When we regularly abandon our own needs, ideas, and values to make others happy, we prioritize their worth over ours.

Shifting out of this habit involves creating healthy boundaries—or limits—with others and expressing those boundaries when necessary. We allow them to have their opinions, feelings, and needs while also allowing ourselves to have our own. This can involve saying no, or it can mean offering a different perspective. It can also mean better self-care if your environment demands too much of you.

By creating healthy boundaries, we learn to feel a sense of separateness that can coexist within a larger field of connectedness in our lives.

9. Develop real empathy for others

While some of us over-prioritize the needs of others, some of us focus too much on our own needs, feelings, preferences, and impulses. We tune out our environment and focus primarily on ourselves (egotism). While some of this can be functional and can serve as the foundation for a healthy psyche and support us not to be confluent, it's a form of selfishness when habitually practiced. In the extreme, we can be viewed as arrogant or uninterested in others.

It's critical to develop real empathy for the feelings of other people, for how we affect them, and for what they need from us. Real empathy involves getting curious about why and how others view the world. It involves trying to see things from their perspective and learning to find the truth of that experience within us. It means seeing people as the whole human beings that they are—and not simply as a "means to an end" in us getting our work done.

Leaders who learn to look beyond themselves and develop deeper empathy are often the most compelling, since they demonstrate that they care about others. When we develop and exercise empathy, we're more likely to create relationships built on trust, compassion, sincerity, and respect.

10. Speak truth with care

Many of us have learned to avoid telling the truth, either because the truth is inconvenient or because we anticipate resistance or loss. Little white lies or vague ways of speaking can become habitual. We find creative ways to avoid difficult conversations in which we disagree (deflection).

However, it's important to learn to tolerate the discomfort of speaking truthfully and build a muscle around being honest. We must learn, with practice, that we are actually bigger than any one experience, including one of discomfort. Put most simply, we must learn to speak truth with care.

When we don't speak truthfully, we deprive others of knowing what we think and feel, which is a betrayal of our own needs. But when we speak truth with care, we respect ourselves and others as well.

Speaking truthfully doesn't mean sharing every random thought in our head. Rather, it's about using a kind and respectful tone, acting with consideration for the person to whom we speak, and conveying the truth of what we want to say. It means communicating clearly and honestly at the same time.

11. Find your own voice

At some point in our lives, often with the assistance of psychotherapy or coaching, many of us realize the extent to which we are products of our upbringing and social/cultural conditioning. There's nothing wrong with this; it's part of the human experience known as the "socialized mind" in Robert Kegan's Theory of Adult Development. It's a necessary stage in our mental and psychological evolution as adults, but we need to find our own voice if we wish to mature and *grow up*.

It can be difficult to find our own voice, which may be faint at first, amid the noise of what we were taught, what our parents believe, or what others communicated to us (explicitly or implicitly) about what is true.

But by being introspective and mindful, we can learn to stand on our own two feet as human beings and adults. We learn to distinguish our own voice and values versus those of our parents or, for that matter, the values of the society and culture that surround us (introjects). In our experience, individuals who find their voice can more fully step into their own unique and authentic way of leading others, based not on outside values but on what they know about themselves.

12. Be the adult in the room

According to Transactional Analysis theory, we all consist of three primary states of consciousness: Parent, Adult, and Child. In any given moment, we are likely operating from one of these states. Until we bring awareness to it, we unconsciously act out these roles as we have learned them. We also unwittingly draw others into our "game." Being the adult in the room is an invitation to show up as the most mature part of ourselves, as often as possible.

Sometimes we are drawn to being in charge, and we think we must tell others what to do. In this state, we are likely to try to control others—meaning we are in Parent state. Some degree of this state can be functional, but only on a limited basis and mostly in our real-life roles as parents. (And even then, it's best used sparingly).

Other times, we show up as a younger, more vulnerable, fragile (or playful) part of our psyche. When we are in Child state, we may frighten more easily, we may be intimidated by others whom we perceive as stronger than us, and we may use a child's method of dealing with a difficult experience—either hiding or acting out—to get what we want. We may try to manipulate others to get our needs met without being direct. Or we may gossip, complain, or tell ourselves we are the victim of our circumstances since we feel like a child in those moments.

Being the adult in the room means functioning from our most evolved and "highest" Self, the Adult who is guided by maturity, inner wisdom, confidence, and trust. This part of us takes responsibility for our actions, demonstrates consistency and dependability in relationships, and tries not to get into power struggles or dramas with others.

When we practice being the adult in the room, we also don't make others into authority figures that we will rebel against or treat them as children we need to discipline (projection). We show up with our own deepest level of maturity, and we invite others to do the same.

13. Be kind to yourself

Being a human being is not easy; being a professional human being is less easy. We may think we want to more collegial, but then we end up competing hard with our colleagues to advocate for a decision to be made in our favor. We may believe we want to have that difficult conversation with our boss, but we feel frightened and we avoid it. To support all of the other practices here, one of the most fundamental is the need to be kind to yourself.

Being kind to yourself might look different on different days or for different people. For some of us, it's about doing things regularly that we enjoy doing—prioritizing our joy and pleasure, because if we are feeling good, then it's easier to be generous. For others, being kind may involve saying positive things to ourselves on a regular basis—things like "you got this!" or "I can see how hard you're working" or "you are enough." By saying kind things to ourselves, we are essentially stepping in to parent and love ourselves—usually this is most needed by a younger part of ourselves that needs attention and acceptance.

The Buddha said, "You can search the world over and you will find no one who is more deserving of your kindness and well-wishing than you yourself." If our only practice for a while is to become more self-aware and to accept ourselves for who we are in this moment, we would consider that a great success.

> > > < < <

Growing Up at Work, it should be noted, is not an exhaustive instruction manual. Nor is it meant to be. It's possible, even likely, we may have missed something along the way in our effort to synthesize many strands of experience into a cogent set of practices aimed at professional evolution and personal growth.

As these practices make clear, whatever is unresolved in one's emotional or psychological life has a reliable way of manifesting in how we relate to others. This can be especially thorny if we possess power or influence over people at work. So, while we invite everyone to read our book, we especially invite leaders to consider what *growing up* could mean for them, since they have an outsized effect on others.

We believe that if you truly want to *grow up at work* then these lessons will support and accelerate your goal. They sit at the intersection of psychotherapy, coaching, leadership development, and spiritual growth. All are critical to greater maturity and self-wisdom.

We also recognize that change can happen in many ways. You can do this work on your own and be introspective, which we strongly encourage. We know that change is supported when it's done with a partner, so we also encourage you to use this book in conjunction with your own coaching or therapy, or in dialogue with a trusted friend.

By absorbing the lessons of our clients and practicing the foundational steps toward transformation, we hope you experience a more meaningful and healthy life at work and home—and continue to pursue a lifelong commitment to learning and growth.

Glossary of Terms

WE'RE SHARING OUR EXPERIENCES COACHING our clients
and the lessons to be learned without overloading their stories with complex psychological terms and jargon. We do, however, need to refer to
certain terms and concepts to illuminate important issues and for you
to better understand the thinking behind our work. It may help to review
these terms in advance and use them for future reference, as needed,
as you find parallels with your own experiences in the workplace, and
even at home.

Adult Development Theory

Developed by US developmental Harvard University psychologist and
author Robert Kegan, this theory outlines the stages of adult development and how shifts from one stage to another are marked by what
shapes our worldview and our sense of self, as well as how we make
meaning in our lives. The shift from socialized mind (characterized by
a worldview shaped largely by social/cultural conditioning) to one of
self-authoring mind (marked by an experience of *choice* about the values and beliefs that guide us) is a theoretical underpinning of this book
and a shift that is well-supported through coaching and psychotherapy. (It should be noted that many other adult development theories

exist—including Erikson, Jung, and Torbert, among others. But for the sake of our book, we will lean on Kegan's model most heavily.) Kegan's work later evolved to include Lisa Laskow Lahey and their "immunity to change" model.

Co-creation

A central concept in Gestalt therapy that suggests each of us plays a role in co-creating our experience of reality; we all contribute to the dynamics in our lives. While it's tempting to find fault in others, seeing how we co-create means we take responsibility for whatever dynamic we find ourselves in—including difficult or painful situations. (This is in contrast to trauma, where co-creation is not usually a useful or accurate frame.) Understanding *our role* in a dynamic requires emotional honesty, maturity, and self-responsibility.

Conflict avoidance

This is a habitual behavior that avoids open conflict or disagreement with others. Typically fear-based, it is often the result of how we were raised and socialized.

Confluence

Confluence is the chronic habit of going along with others, usually the result of overriding one's own limits or boundaries.

Creative adjustment

According to Gestalt theory, this is a creative and unconscious coping mechanism we develop early on in our lives to deal with a painful or difficult situation. In psychoanalytic terms, creative adjustments might also be called defenses. We use creative adjustments to deal with the circumstances we encounter; while these are often unconscious (think of someone who has a habit of smiling when uncomfortable), we sometimes develop creative adjustments with conscious awareness (e.g., choosing to postpone a difficult conversation until a better moment).

Cycle of experience (also contact cycle)

A central tenet of Gestalt psychotherapy, this is a simple model for understanding how we are essentially built as human beings to become aware of our needs, to respond to our needs, and to move on once those needs are met. Early on in our lives, many of us form certain habits when we find our efforts to have our needs met are unacknowledged or unsuccessful.

Deflection

This is a way in which we avoid a difficult experience or emotion and find a replacement for it, often to take the heat out of a situation. One common example can be making a joke in a moment of discomfort.

Drama triangle

A concept originated by author and psychiatrist Stephen Karpman, who used the terms oppressors, victims, and rescuers to describe the roles we unconsciously play in unhealthy interpersonal dynamics that resemble a triangle of roles. The Conscious Leadership Group has more recently renamed these roles as villain, victim, and hero to similarly describe the way we fall into unhealthy dynamics with each other. These dynamics are marked by drama and the failure to take responsibility for our experiences or our choices.

Egotism

In this orientation toward the world we assume that our needs and experience are central, and in doing so, we fail to see the needs of others. In its non-pathological form, egotism can be seen as a slowing down of immediate contact with others to allow for more useful contact when we are ready to reengage.

False self

Developed by English psychoanalyst D.W. Winnicott, this concept involves our putting on an artificial front for others to be perceived as acceptable. This front is in contrast to our true Self, which is more authentic and respectful of our needs.

Gestalt therapy

From the German word for "shape," "whole," or "composition," Gestalt therapy is a humanistic form of psychotherapy grounded in the present-moment experience of the client and the therapist. It was developed by Fritz Perls (in collaboration with his wife, Laura Perls) in the 1950s and 1960s, and one of its primary aims is to help clients achieve greater wholeness and integration in their lives. Laura Perls once described Gestalt therapy as "experiential, experimental, and existential" in nature.

Imposter syndrome

This is a highly common experience that involves someone feeling like a fake or a fraud. It is usually accompanied by an impending sense of being "found out."

Individuation

Discussed by psychologists like Margaret Mahler and others, this is a process that describes an emotional shift or moving away from parental expectations and beliefs as we become mature adults with our own dreams, aspirations, and lives.

Interruption in contact

Interruptions in contact are ways in which our natural needs and impulses have been muted or altered by early experiences. Over time, these interruptions become our habitual ways of being in the world, but they keep us from what we actually need for wholeness. An interruption in contact is usually characterized by being chronic, out of our awareness, and anachronistic. Common Gestalt interruptions include introjection, retroflection, confluence, deflection, and egotism. At their essence, interruptions in contact are a form of creative adjustment made in response to our experience in the world. (See also, creative adjustment.)

Introjection

This is a belief we live by and the ideas that shape our sense of self and identity. It also represents our worldview, which is usually taken in whole from our environment, upbringing, and family systems. Introjects often come in the form of "shoulds" that we believe about how to behave, communicate, relate, or lead.

Learning mindset

This orientation toward life assumes that everything is an opportunity for learning and growth—in contrast to a "fixed" mindset that assumes growth is not possible, especially by a certain age.

Making the unconscious conscious

This is one of the primary goals of psychotherapy (and some coaching), which is to bring awareness to the beliefs, values, assumptions, and experiences that drive us. Until we bring the unconscious into consciousness, we are usually on some form of "autopilot" in life.

Overfunctioning

From the world of family therapy, this is the concept that some members of dysfunctional families or other systems function more than is their "share" and create opportunities for others in the system to do less. Over time, this creates an unhealthy pattern or dance between overfunctioners and underfunctioners.

Paradoxical theory of change

Made famous by Gestalt therapist Arnold Beisser's essay, this is the idea that only when one's present experience is fully accepted is it possible for change to actually occur.

Parent-Adult-Child (PAC) model

From the work of Transactional Analysis, this model holds that in any given moment we are usually in one of three forms of consciousness—Parent, Adult, or Child. The Parent state is characterized by an authoritarian attitude; the Child state is characterized by less emotional maturity—often a regressed psychological state; the Adult state is reflective of our wisdom and maturity.

Projection

A projection is an interruption in contact whereby we imagine that our fears and wishes are possessed by others. In other words, we place our emotions or beliefs "onto" others.

Psychological safety

Introduced by US leadership and organizational learning scholar Amy C. Edmondson, and later studied by Google, psychological safety is a sense of emotional security that gives rise to better morale, productivity, and creativity in the workplace.

Retroflection

Retroflection is an interruption in contact whereby we essentially do to ourselves what others did to us—or what we wished others had done. It's also the action of attacking ourselves when we would like to attack the other. When we retroflect, we interrupt our excitement and seek to control our experience instead of allowing a feeling to emerge and organically engaging with our environment. Healthy retroflection can be controlling an unhealthy impulse (for instance, not saying something hurtful), but it often can take the form of self-attack or self-criticism or it can involve holding back our natural enthusiasm.

Self-authoring mind

This is the fourth state of mind in Robert Kegan's Adult Development Theory, which is marked by a shift from one's worldview being informed largely by social conditioning to one that is derived from self-examination, introspection, and choice.

Socialized mind

This is the third stage of Kegan's Adult Development Theory, which reflects a shift from a mindset predominated by one's own needs for control or significance to one in which one's needs are central and paramount to a worldview that is characterized by socialization and fitting in. In this stage, our beliefs, values, and choices are deeply conditioned by our environment.

Transactional Analysis

This psychoanalytic theory and method of therapy, originated by Eric Berne, analyzes social interactions to determine the ego state of whoever is communicating (Parent, Child, or Adult) as a basis for understanding behavior.

Transference

A central concept in psychoanalysis, this is a pattern of interacting with, or reacting to, others as if they were significant figures from our early childhood, like parents, siblings, or teachers. We transfer our past attitudes and feelings onto a present person like our manager or work colleagues, and in so doing, we fail to see that our relationship is more reflective of *our past* than the present.

Underfunctioning

This dynamic involves doing disproportionately less than one's share—in a family or in an organization—often giving rise to another person in the system having to do more, or overfunctioning. We may not realize consciously that we are contributing to a system where we take on one of these roles until we become aware of it.

Unfinished Gestalt

This refers to an unresolved situation or dynamic in need of resolution. Without realizing it, many of our unhealthy patterns in life are informed by an incomplete or unfinished Gestalt. One common example of this dynamic can be grief that we have avoided or resisted feeling.

Chapter 1

I Feel Like an Imposter

WITHIN TWO MINUTES OF SITTING down with me, Julia burst into tears.

"I don't know if I'm right for this job. I don't know if I can do it. I don't know if I'm succeeding at this," she said, looking at me intently, her body hunched over. "I'm afraid I'm not doing a very good job, and this isn't going as well as I had hoped."

She caught herself. "I'm so sorry I'm crying."

This wasn't the Julia I knew. I had first met her when she was a student in my leadership program. The kind of person who lights up a room, Julia was naturally full of energy, funny, and sweet. She managed to be simultaneously charming and authentic, a combination that led to her becoming a great favorite in class. She made friends easily.

After graduating from college, Julia, a white Jewish woman in her late twenties, got a job with a nonprofit educational advocacy organization and rose rapidly through the ranks. Academically gifted and driven, but not super-ambitious, she'd take an opportunity if it presented itself and felt right. A chance to move to New York? *OK, I'll do that.* Move into a more senior position? *OK, I'll do that.* She took things on mostly because they were there to be taken on and because she was a curious, bright person.

I offer all of my students a one-on-one coaching session as part of the leadership program I teach. Julia was one of the first to avail herself of this session, so here she was, this funny, bright, highly capable person—someone whom I knew was very smart based on my class—yet within two minutes of sitting down with me, she was in tears. She had been promoted consistently throughout her career and the only feedback she ever received was glowing, but her head was in her hands as she told me she was terrible at her job.

"I bet everyone at work is convinced I can't do my job," she said. "They're probably sorry they hired me. It's only a matter of time before they figure out that I really don't know what I'm doing."

What was going on here? Where was she getting this message?

Imposter syndrome

"Imposter syndrome," where you continually doubt your achievements and live with the fear of being exposed as a fraud, is a deeply familiar experience for many people I've worked with, including successful professionals and leaders, across all ages and industries.

With Julia, the impact of what she was going through wasn't really visible on the surface. She was such a buoyant, effervescent personality that most of the people in her life were completely unaware of what was going on inside of her. But the pain and isolation were very real—affecting her mood, her relationships, her sleep.

My approach with Julia, as we'll see throughout this book with other clients, was to "make the unconscious conscious," which is to bring awareness to the beliefs, values, assumptions, and experiences that drive us. I sought to unpack the *thinking* that was leading to her suffering and hampering her development as a leader. I needed to hear exactly what Julia believed about herself. What was the story she was hearing in her head? Whose story was that? What was drowning out all of the positive feedback and leaving her instead with the terrible sense of being a failure?

A feeling can often be traced back to the thought that caused it. While some feelings seem to come from our gut, and those feelings may very well be based in trauma or pain from our past, our feelings often originate from a story we tell about ourselves—thoughts that we don't even know we are thinking that give rise to negative feelings. For example: *I'm telling myself that my coworkers think I'm lazy because I told them I couldn't help out with a project. When I tell myself this story, I feel sad and ashamed.* There's the thought, then *boom!* there's the feeling.

As Julia spoke, as we explored her thoughts, it quickly became obvious that there was more than one voice in the room—two in particular. There was the part of Julia that was suffering because she felt like she was an imposter, but this process all started because there was another part of Julia, an "inner critic" that was telling Julia over and over again that she wasn't doing a good job. And that voice was informed by an imagined perception of how others viewed her. The voice of the receiver, the victim, was largely silent, taking in all of this abuse—it hadn't been clear to Julia that she was actually berating *herself*.

The good news is that by simply identifying imposter syndrome as a common thought pattern, and by giving it a name, we can start to work with it.

"Do you recognize part of what's going on here as a phenomenon called imposter syndrome?" I asked Julia. "Does that sound right to you?"

Asking this question is the first step toward breaking down the sense of isolation that often comes with imposter syndrome. The belief that everyone else sees you as a fraud, combined with the idea that everyone else around you must know what they are doing, is a very unpleasant way of suffering and feeling alone.

"It could be. That's really interesting," she said, her blue eyes widening. We smiled at each other. "I hadn't thought of it that way."

Exploring the voices inside

To understand why we are suffering, it's necessary to explore exactly what's going on inside of us. With Julia, I wanted to hear the voice of her inner critic to know what it was saying and to understand the effect it was having on her. So I invited Julia to speak from that voice. What exactly was she telling herself?

"You're such a fake," she spat, "you're such a phony. Everyone knows you don't know how to do this job, and it's only a matter of time before you're really found out by everyone."

What was happening here, according to "Gestalt therapy," is called an "interruption in contact," which involves how early experiences mute or alter our natural needs and impulses. It essentially describes the different ways we unwittingly block our flow, our energy, our excitement, our love of life.

This interruption in contact was actually two interruptions in one. First off, Julia was "projecting," whereby she was imagining the thoughts of her colleagues and that they had a negative set of perceptions of her. The second interruption here is called "retroflection." This is where *we attack ourselves*, either in the way that others have attacked us or in the way we wish we could attack others, or to try to force ourselves to be a particular way in the world.

After hearing from the part of Julia that was creating the attack, I asked if she was aware that there was another part of her that was actually *receiving* this message. In essence, the receiver of the messages is our inner victim—the part that receives the inner attack.

"How does this part feel?" I asked. "And what, if anything, do you want to say in response?"

While she felt sad to hear these critical words about herself, she agreed with what the critic had to say.

"The critic is right. I really am not good my job, and everyone knows it."

Take back your eyes and stand up to your inner critic

As we began our work together, I started by discussing the psychological process of "projection" with Julia. Many of us spend a lot of our mental energy projecting onto others as if they are a blank movie screen. We often tend to project our fears onto others—and sometimes we project our wishes, too. We don't even realize we are projecting, and we also feel quite convinced that whatever we are projecting is accurate.

In Julia's case, I wanted to start by helping her see this first distortion that was getting in her way: She was seeing herself through her imagination of what others thought of her and she didn't even realize that this was what she was doing. Step one for Julia was to *take back her eyes* and realize that *she* was the one who was creating the voice in her head—no one else.

Once Julia realized that it was part of herself that was imagining the worst, we looked next at what she was *doing* with that information. She was attacking herself with it. So, just as you would coach a child being bullied on the playground, I began to fortify that victimized, quiescent part of Julia's psyche. Standing up to your inner critic—something we also refer to as *making peace with the bully*—is about exchanging the voice of the victim with the voice of strength. I encourage my clients to get in touch with how they would respond if these mean things were being said to someone they cared about.

I began coaching Julia to defend herself by proxy, to think of it as defending someone else.

I asked Julia, "What would you say if this bully was talking to a friend of yours? How would you react?" The truth is that it's much easier for us to stand up to a bully if they're bullying somebody that we love.

"I would tell them to stop," she said, without hesitation. "I would tell them that this was unacceptable, that this was *not* OK. That what they were saying wasn't even true."

Velcro and Teflon

It's said that negative thoughts are like Velcro. They tend to stick. As human beings, we have a knack for believing, and ruminating on, negative thoughts about ourselves, and we feel bad as a result.

This was certainly true for Julia. She was in the habit of telling herself that she wasn't good enough at her job, that she was an imposter, and as a result, she told herself that she was a failure. This thought pattern was on a loop in her head and had a "sticky" quality in her consciousness.

Meanwhile, positive thoughts tend to be like Teflon. They often don't stick. Someone tells us we do something really well and we just think, yeah, well, I'm not so sure . . . We write them off.

The reality was that Julia was in receipt of plenty of positive feedback—there was no shortage of people telling her she was doing a great job, but she had trouble believing it.

Sometimes we have to borrow the confidence others have in us and see ourselves through their eyes. People often see in us what we can't see in ourselves, and it can take deliberate effort to appreciate something positive about ourselves and to *decide* to be affected by it.

Julia began working on trying to be affected by the positivity around her and by the praise that her colleagues were expressing toward her. This took a lot of practice. It's not easy to take a mental concept and turn it into something that's lived in the body, to see that you have talents and gifts and to recognize that you can live them.

During one of our next sessions, Julia told me about a curriculum she was working on, and I used this opportunity to put my observations into play.

"Julia, that's such an innovative way of putting theory into practice," I said. "I find you so imaginative."

"Thanks, but anyone could have done that," she responded.

"Let's pause," I said. "What just happened? Did you notice you just brushed me off? You just deflected that positive thing I shared about you being creative."

She looked surprised. "Deflection" is a way in which we avoid a difficult experience or emotion and find a replacement for it.

"How familiar is that?" I asked.

"Quite familiar."

"I wonder if I could say it again to you and instead of your just moving past it, I wonder if, as an experiment, you could just let yourself be affected by what I said," I told her. "Just hear my compliment and feel my positive words."

I repeated what I had previously said, and a few seconds passed.

"What was that like?" I asked.

"That was interesting," she said. "I'm feeling some tingling in my stomach."

"I noticed your shoulders relaxed, too."

"That's true," she responded. "Yeah, I was touched by what you said."

This took a lot of practice. It's not easy to take a mental concept and turn it into something that's lived in the body, to see that you have talents and gifts and to recognize that you can live them.

Over time, Julia could start to say, "I think I understand why I've been promoted." She could begin to appreciate the things she liked about her job. She could chair a high-level meeting at the mayor's office, and in her mind, she could hear the voice that used to do nothing but accept the criticism say, "I can do this, I'm good at this."

Julia also started a journaling practice to support the coaching pro-cess. Journaling can also be really helpful in this process, as there's only so much you can accomplish in a fifty-minute session every other week, and journaling accelerates self-inquiry. Instead of simply feeling bad, we can explore how the pain is being created in our psyche. We notice and track self-talk. You might think, *I've no idea what I'm doing here*, and instead of giving way instantly to the feeling that this can generate, you stop and label the thought: *This is critical self-talk.*

Techniques like these allowed Julia to separate herself from the story she was telling herself. With time, and with support in our sessions, she also practiced responding to her critical self-talk with compassion, love, reason, and balance.

"Yes, I am new to this role, and I am still learning, but that doesn't make me any different than anyone else who's new to a role," she said. "I can see how much I am trying, and others do, too. Why not try to just trust in that a little more?"

Getting curious about the inner critic

In addition to helping Julia fortify her inner victim and learn to take in positive support, I worked with her to explore her inner critic and to encourage her to do the same. We started examining questions like: Where did this inner critic come from? When did it start? Why was she pushing herself in this particular way?

I also wondered if the voice of her inner critic reminded her of some-one. In some cases—not so much with Julia—but frequently, the voice is the replica of a parent. The person is doing to themselves what was done to them.

One of the things that can be especially illuminating when we get curious about our inner critic is to better understand how old we were when this part of ourselves developed. While not an exact science, many clients have a sense of when this part of themselves emerged, and this was true for Julia as well.

As it turns out, Julia's parents, as well as her teachers, gave her a lot of attention for being smart and successful at school. Her parents were never critical of her, she recalled.

"They thought that the sun revolved around me," she said. "They told me I was the smartest, most talented kid, and I really came to believe that. My teachers gave me a ton of praise, too."

"How do you think that impacted you?"

She thought a moment. "My identity until I was a young adult was really around being the A student," she said, "being a good girl, being responsible."

As a result, her inner voice reinforced this desire to win approval and retain her identity in the world as a smart person, a solid performer, and someone who was willing to take on any challenge. Gradually, it became more ruthless, holding her to higher and higher standards. This part of Julia didn't take well to not knowing everything, and I took notice.

"That's so interesting," I said. "So, this voice didn't come from your parents?"

"No."

"And it didn't come from your teachers?"

"No."

"It seems like it came from inside of you."

"Yeah, I guess it did."

"Any sense of when it started?" I asked.

Julia paused, and her eyes welled up with tears.

"I think it was when I was a kid, probably eleven or twelve. It's been with me a long time," she said. She began to smile. "I don't know why I'm getting so emotional about this right now."

"I'm not sure, either," I said, passing her a tissue. "Let's look more closely at this."

With reflection and through coaching, Julia came to realize that her inner critic, the part that was continually attacking her, was a child. That part of Julia understandably wanted approval, but she also had developed a simple equation that led to that sense of approval and safety. If she performed well and she felt completely confident, she concluded that she was lovable and safe.

In contrast, if Julia was less certain about herself, she was walking in uncharted territory and her inner critic responded with fear and self-attack. Her inner child didn't know what to do with the fact that, indeed, adulthood, and professional life, includes many moments of *not knowing*, *learning*, even *failure*. These experiences enable us to grow, if we are open, but with an inner critic monitoring the situation all the time, they are also ripe for self-attack.

Addressing the empty chair

One of the ways in which I work as a coach is doing "experiments" with my clients, and a powerful Gestalt experiment is called the "empty chair," where we speak either to a part of ourselves or to someone else. I've done it with clients both in person and via live video. In Julia's case, I invited her to converse with her inner critic and to explore this part of herself.

I always have an empty chair in the office, so clients don't usually think too much about it. Julia didn't, either, until I asked her if she would mind if we did a little experiment. (If I'm working with a client during an online session, due to COVID-19 or not, I sometimes ask the client to set up an empty chair in their room to assist with our process.)

She looked at me quizzically, a bit fearful and intrigued all at once.

"The empty chair is here by design," I explained. "In Gestalt-informed work, we believe that this chair can help us have conversations in the moment with either parts of ourselves or people in our lives, and we can just sort of see what emerges."

I let her absorb this for a moment, then continued, "I'm wondering what it would be like for you and me to talk to this part of you. Would you be willing to do this experiment?"

"OK," she said, and I could tell she was trying to be a good sport.

"Before you get up and try to feel this part of you, I'd like for you to look over at that empty chair and imagine your inner critic. What does this part of you look like? What do you see?"

Her eyes squinted, as if trying to focus on a distant image. Some people see it quickly; for others, it takes awhile.

"I see an eleven-year-old girl," Julia said. "She has a stern look on her face, and her arms are crossed."

"That's interesting," I said. "How are you affected by her?"

"I'm kind of uncomfortable around her. She's staring at me."

"Now, would you be willing to get up and sit in her seat?"

Julia got up slowly and walked over to the chair. She hesitated for a second, then sat down.

"Just let yourself be affected by this," I said.

"My stomach just sank," she said. "I'm feeling kind of sad and angry over here."

"OK, I know this part might be tricky. Can you imagine embodying this critic, who is actually not a separate person but a part of you? Can you look over at the other part of Julia and talk to her? What would you tell her?"

"I'm here to make sure that you're doing your job correctly, and you've got to work hard," Julia said. "If you don't work hard, you're not going to succeed, and I'm afraid people are going to think you're a failure. You've got to be the best."

"Those are pretty stark terms," I said. "Very black and white."

I invited her to return to her original chair.

"How are you feeling? What did you notice about her voice, and her words?" I asked.

"She speaks in such simple terms. She sees me like a child would."

"What might you say to this inner critic?"

"You're being too simplistic, and it's not fair. Life isn't like that, especially adult life," Julia said, feeling emboldened. She sat up straighter in her chair. "I'm learning. I'm making mistakes. And there's nothing wrong with that."

I cannot overstate the importance of ongoing awareness in this kind of transformation. Think of the psyche as a container. When you're not aware of the inner critic, its voice can take over. But by noticing it, it doesn't sound quite as loud or half as credible. Eckhart Tolle, a prominent spiritual teacher, puts it like this: "When you make your unconscious motivations conscious, you immediately see how absurd they are. Awareness is the greatest agent for change."

Julia and I were able to confirm our hypothesis that the critic was a young part of Julia focused on protecting herself. With her increased awareness, she came to see that the part of her that created pain was also a part that deserved love and attention—ideally, *from Julia herself* as an adult.

The truth and the lie

One thing I've realized over the years is that there is both a *truth* and a *lie* at the heart of imposter syndrome. The lie—the inner critic's continual assertion that we are a failure, a phony—we've already talked about. It's usually a way of trying to keep ourselves safe that is based in fear, but in essence the lie we tell ourselves is this: *We should already know everything and if we don't, we're a failure.*

The truth is that none of us knows everything. We are all on a learning curve. This is particularly true when we take on a new role or are promoted into a position of authority. It is at this point that Julia was most vulnerable to the voice of her critic, because there were, of course, things that she needed to work on. For instance, she didn't have a great deal of experience in operations, a new aspect of her role.

Julia also frequently had difficulty when it came to big decisions that affected other people. In one particular case, she needed to decide whether a certain academic subject should be made mandatory on the curriculum—a decision that she knew would affect thousands of kids. She was paralyzed by indecision. The anxiety this generated was exacerbated by one of her direct reports who saw what was happening and challenged her authority.

"I don't know what to do right now. I'm so torn about whether to make this decision one way or the other. This is exactly what I meant by not knowing what I'm doing. A good leader would know how to make this decision," Julia told me. "My staff member is so much more decisive than me, and she's getting really annoyed by my lack of leadership on this, and I don't blame her."

We are at our most vulnerable at moments like these, since it is now more than ever that the critical voice carries a certain moral authority.

How do you separate the lie from the truth when they are so entangled?

The hallmark of the lie is that it is monolithic. It is nonspecific. *You are a failure, a phony, a fraud. Everyone knows more than you.*

The truth, by contrast, is more nuanced, more specific. Because of this, it's far more amenable to specific solutions. We can distill what we want to learn and practice, what we want to refine in our new role, asking ourselves:

- Are there classes I need to take?

- Could I benefit from mentoring?

- Is there a professional development program I could access?

Is this what I want?

I've also come to see that imposter syndrome may sometimes speak to the fact that maybe this *isn't* the best match between your interests and skills and what the job is asking of you, and there's nothing wrong with considering this possibility—though ideally without self-attack. Experiencing imposter syndrome can be helpful in that it does sometimes force you to ask serious questions.

- Is this the right role for me?

- Am I enjoying this?

- Does it resonate with who I am and my natural strengths?

- If I'm not good at something, is it something I *want* to get better at?

These are legitimate questions, which demand reflection, and they are qualitatively different from the shrill voice of the inner critic, which seeks only to insist that you are putting one over on everyone.

It's also true that sometimes a pinch of imposter syndrome can help us stay realistic and grounded—as kind of an antidote to arrogance. Realizing we don't know everything can reveal humility—the foundation of all virtues, according to Confucius—and humility, in my opinion, is something every leader needs. Note, too, that the spur of imposter syndrome prompted Julia to look at her own growth, both professional and personal. Growing into a sense of self-trust and self-confidence means that we also learn to lead from a place of deep connection to ourselves. We become authentic; we feel more like ourselves.

To get Julia to that place, we examined her decision-making skills and sought supports that broke the neurotic spiral, allowing her to move away from a place of shame and self-attack, and grow in the way that she needed. She began to trust her judgment without shame and started to inform big decisions that relied on data and consultation with others.

Dealing with imposter syndrome in this way allowed Julia to be more present, to break the connection with a mental narrative that was not real. This also enabled her to become a better coach and a better manager because she was that much more empathic to how some of her staff might be feeling in starting a new role.

The magic of the moment

Julia and I worked together for a year. Over that time, we saw a gradual reduction in her suffering. She became lighter, happier. She had less trouble sleeping.

There was more flow in her life, more joy, more confidence. She came to realize that her struggle with feeling like an imposter felt both personal and universal. She practiced regularly "taking back her eyes" to discern what she actually felt about herself and her work instead of imagining that others were thinking the worst. She caught herself as she was about to go on the self-attack, and she stopped it.

She also enjoyed additional promotions at work and discovered her capacity to recognize and accept the admiration of those around her. Near the end of our work, she was selected as one of the few industry leaders asked to address a prestigious conference on educational advocacy.

"I'm so excited about it," she told me.

"Wow, that's fabulous," I said. "It feels to me you're being recognized for the great work you're doing."

We smiled and laughed together, celebrating her accomplishments.

"No one thinks I'm a failure," she said. And finally, she believed it.

► REFLECTIONS ◄

- Through whose "eyes" do I see myself?

- What do I expect myself to know by now, and why?

- How would I know how to do this without learning it?

- How does it affect me when I tell myself I'm an imposter? Would I talk to anyone else like that?

- What would make me feel less like an imposter? What do I need to learn and practice to feel equipped for this role, this job, this challenge?

- What supportive words can I offer myself if I'm feeling scared or insecure?

► PRACTICES ◄

- Distinguish your thoughts from your feelings. If you're feeling bad, stop and investigate the story you're telling yourself.

- Come back to the present. Name what you're seeing, feeling, hearing, tasting. Get back into your body. Exercise or meditate, whatever it takes to get out of your head.

- If you become aware of your inner critic, practice becoming aware of your critical voice and also practice standing up to your critic. Journaling can be a great tool for this, and you can do it as if you're writing dialogue between two different characters.

- Say kind words to yourself on a daily basis. Talk about what you appreciate about yourself. Practice talking to yourself the way you would talk to somebody you love. You can do this in a mirror, in a journal, or by looking at a picture of yourself at a younger age.

► **EXPERIMENTS** ◄

- Branch out! Take a class or seek support or mentoring for something you don't know how to do.

- Take five minutes to talk to yourself out loud about the things you appreciate about yourself. Write down how you feel afterward.

Chapter 2

I'm Their Manager,
but I Want to Be Their Friend

ONE OF MY LONGSTANDING CORPORATE clients is an engineering firm in Minnesota. A reputable and prominent employer in its small town, the firm prides itself on being at the cutting edge of engineering developments and innovation. Many local young people in the area grow up hoping to get the qualifications they need to start a career there.

Dave, a white man in his late thirties, was no exception. He had joined the company after completing his master's degree in engineering, and several of his old high school friends had followed the same route. At work, they renewed old friendships, spending time together in their lunch breaks and after work.

Dave quickly proved himself to be a potentially brilliant engineer, with a quick mind and a creative streak that led him to seek out new and unusual solutions to apparently straightforward problems. Several years into his tenure, when his manager retired, Dave applied for the promotion and got it. The company saw Dave as talented, able, and energetic and as being clearly popular with his colleagues. They saw real leadership potential in him and hoped he would quickly grow into the role—one that required him to manage his former peers.

But, after a successful start, the company began to feel that Dave wasn't developing into the leader they had hoped he could be, and they approached me to coach him.

Dave's senior manager, Andrew, a thoughtful and serious man, left no doubt that they had a serious problem on their hands.

"We're beginning to feel that he's not providing the leadership the team needs," Andrew said.

He paused and stared down at his hands for a moment.

"I think he'd be amazed to find that he's not universally liked. He's got a group of friends that he seems very close to, but he hasn't earned everyone's respect—not yet," he said. "We also don't feel that he's become a full member of the management team. It's as if he still sees himself as being one of the boys rather than as a manager. I've raised these issues with him in our meetings, but I haven't seen any real changes in his behavior."

Andrew went on to say that he felt Dave didn't sufficiently challenge his team. And, because Dave was so tight with his circle of friends, he shared concerns with them about whether particular targets he had set as a manager were reasonable, which undermined their confidence of success.

Andrew also expressed concerns about whether Dave was involving the women in his team as much as the men.

"Dave seems more comfortable with the guys," he said. "I see them in the cafeteria together or heading off for a beer after work. I don't want the women in our team to feel excluded, and I'm afraid this is sending a bad message."

As I would discover, his fears were well founded.

Easygoing but exclusive

For the first coaching session, I traveled to Minnesota to meet Dave. He greeted me with a big smile and firm handshake. Dressed in the business casual uniform of a brightly colored polo shirt and khaki trousers, he had a crewcut and an athletic build and seemed confident and slightly bashful at the same time.

"Hey, so nice to meet you," he said. "How was your trip here? Thanks for coming all this way."

I had seen from his resume that Dave played football in college, and there was a photograph on his office wall. It was easy to recognize Dave in the young player grinning happily at the camera, surrounded by his teammates.

Dave knew that I had provided coaching for some of the most senior executives in the company, so he saw the sessions as something of a privilege and a confirmation of their investment in him.

"I was encouraged to hear you've coached some of the executives in our company because when I heard they wanted me to see you, I wondered if I did something wrong," he said, still smiling.

As we continued to talk, it became clear that being "a nice guy" was a core part of his personality. It seemed as if Dave wanted everyone to be his friend, and he hadn't felt the need to change that when he became a manager.

He continued to have lunch in the cafeteria with his old circle of friends, many who now reported to him. He also hung out with them after work from time to time, priding himself on how he was still "one of the guys."

But it was clear there were problems hidden beneath the surface.

The feedback

In most of our coaching assignments, we do some form of assessment to understand how the client is perceived in the workplace. In Dave's case, I spoke with several of his colleagues confidentially about what they considered his strengths to be and where they saw areas for improvement.

The members of Dave's inner circle were, unsurprisingly, highly supportive and overall full of praise. They thought Dave was a great guy, and they clearly hoped that their privileged access to him would help their career prospects as well. Yet even this group, his closest friends, had concerns.

One young man told me that he felt privileged that Dave took him into his confidence about management issues. The trouble was that this blurred the chain of command, confirming Andrew's fears.

"Dave is very honest with us about his own situation and what he needs to achieve, which is great," said the colleague. "But sometimes he lets himself complain about what he's been asked to do. He'll say that he doesn't think some companywide target is achievable or that he thinks the firm is being unreasonable asking us to do this. And that's actually not helpful. It can be a bit demotivating."

He also expressed concerns about Dave's objectivity.

"I can't really complain, but I sense that Dave finds it hard to criticize me," he said. "When we have our performance evaluation sessions, I feel I get off lightly—and I would actually welcome some constructive criticism."

Outside of Dave's circle of close friends, another colleague said it was hard not to feel excluded, even though he didn't necessarily desire a friendship with Dave. Key assignments and promotions tended to go to members of Dave's close circle, he said.

We also made a point of talking to several women on the team. The company for many years had played an active role in bringing more women engineers into the company, working with local schools to encourage girls to consider engineering as a future career option. Dave's leadership team was predominantly male, but nearly one-third of his departmental team were women.

"It's very much, you know, 'the guys,'" said one female team member, using air quotes. "Dave's management style sets up an us-versus-them dynamic when, in fact, together we're a good team."

She mentioned another issue, too. In a recent performance review meeting with Dave, she brought up her concern about a male colleague's patronizing attitude toward women. She was horrified later when one of Dave's close friends mentioned it in conversation with her.

"I'd never discussed this with anyone else, so I knew Dave had talked about it with his friends," she said. "If I tell my manager something, I expect it to be confidential, and I expect it to be dealt with professionally. Now, I don't entirely feel I can trust him."

Inner circles and broken trust

When I suggested to him that the women in his team felt excluded from his circle of friends, he looked confused.

"Well, I . . . I just don't know the women so well," he said. "I mean, they're not—"

"Not what?"

"Uh, they're not my buddies. We're just colleagues," he said, adding, "but we all get along very well."

"Do you think they should be 'buddies'?" I asked.

"No! Well, maybe. I don't know," he said, starting to look confused. "If I start inviting women to lunch with me or whatever, isn't that inappropriate?"

I smiled.

"Inviting them to a candlelit dinner for two would be inappropriate. Inviting them to join you and the boys for a sandwich at lunch or a beer after work is good team-building."

"Have you considered inviting other people to join you? People you don't normally socialize with? Or to create a calendar of meeting up informally with different sets of people?"

"I see what you mean," he said.

I also raised the issue of confidentiality and of Dave's discussing confidential personnel issues with his circle of friends. Dave was indignant.

"Who told you that? What issues?"

I asked him to think carefully about whether it was possible that he ever let information slip to his friends that he had been told in confidence by other team members. He pursed his lips and frowned a little, staring at the floor.

"I'd like to think I don't do that. That would be awful."

"Some of your friends also suggested that you might be too frank and honest with them," I said, sensing his upset and trying to tread carefully. "That you share your concerns about targets and projects. They are flattered you confide in them as friends, but it also makes them a bit demotivated as employees. You know, if Dave thinks this is unachievable, what am I supposed to think?"

"Oh gosh."

"Some of them also suggested that they would welcome some more constructive criticism from you. That they feel you go easy on them because you're quite close."

"Well, I—"

He fell back in his chair.

"I had no idea."

Dave was looking a bit shell-shocked, but he was beginning to engage with the issues.

A habit of going along

As we started getting into the deeper work of coaching, and as Dave's awareness of himself, his habits, and his motivations began to grow, he started to see himself more clearly than before.

What became more apparent was that one of Dave's primary ways of interacting was through "confluence," the chronic habit of going along with others, usually at the expense of one's own limits or boundaries.

Just as we talk about the confluence of two rivers where they merge into one, so too do some people attempt to "merge" with other people as a habitual way of forming relationships, often to avoid conflict. They try to occupy the same space. They are uncomfortable with "otherness," so they attempt to align themselves completely with the other people. They become confluent—an interruption in contact in Gestalt psychotherapy.

Some aspects of confluence can be functional. If we're part of a team, or in a romantic relationship, sometimes we need to subdue elements of our personality in order to get along. But often our confluence with other people comes about as part of an unspoken pact to behave in certain ways and that can lead to simmering feelings of guilt or resentment.

Certainly, we all need to grow and develop as adults to become more effective leaders. But if we just do things to be liked—to please other people to avoid conflict or to protect our self-image—we end up simply reacting to the changing moods, ideas, and feelings of those around us. We become like a leaf in the wind, and we lack the integrity and maturity to be true adults, not to mention more effective leaders. This is also an example of "socialized mind," from Kegan's "Adult Development Theory," a stage during which our identity is determined largely by how we've been socialized to behave.

Over the years, Dave had cultivated the habit of being easygoing and likeable. I invited him to consider why he had this habit. Most of us have such long-formed habits that we don't question why we act in certain ways. I wanted to know how confluence served him, and what it was protecting him from. In Dave's case, it became clear that his need to be friends with people, including those who now reported to him, actually stemmed from a deeper insecurity reaching back to adolescence, a time when everyone is trying to fit in.

Discovering the *why* beneath our habits

I asked Dave about his childhood and his adolescence. Leaning back in his chair, his arms behind his head, he looked up at the ceiling as if searching for words. I realized this was probably the first time in his life he had thought about any of this. I could tell it was a humbling experience.

"Making everyone my friend in high school felt like a form of self-protection," he said.

I paused a moment, then asked, "Who would you be if you weren't likable, popular Dave?"

He looked at me blankly, and that was telling in itself. Blank looks are always interesting. They usually signify that we are coming up against something unconscious within us that we can't easily access and don't fully understand. This can be the step toward real change.

"If I weren't popular, if I weren't liked by everyone, I don't know who I'd be," he said, and I could hear fear in his voice.

It was as if Dave had struck an unspoken pact with other people that this was how it was going to be: Everyone would be his friend and that would protect him from feeling unlikable. It also would enable him to avoid having to form more challenging relationships where not everyone got along.

As we talked, he could see that there were costs to being the likable guy—among others, his habits were making him a less effective manager. And he didn't want that.

Dave was beginning to realize that if it was "lonely at the top," then he had to start becoming more comfortable with being lonely—an experience he had avoided most of his life.

Becoming a better manager

In his role at work, and as a result of his need to be liked and encircled by a group of buddies, Dave began to see that he had been guilty of a kind of favoritism.

He understood more than before that he had treated his inner circle of friends differently from the rest of the team and that his open, friendly relationship with them had led him to be too open and even indiscreet. He saw that other people felt excluded—and were, and that even some of his close friends felt they were getting preferential treatment. He also realized that he had been more comfortable with "the boys" and that forging an adult relationship with women was still a challenge for him.

As Dave realized that some of the team thought that he had behaved poorly, he realized that he had not been putting himself in their shoes or seeing things through their eyes. His assumption that he was universally liked, and that other people were essentially friends-in-waiting, prevented him from seeing other people as they truly were, because to do so would mean that Dave would have to deal with the other person as being "other" and therefore a threat to Dave's self-image. But that capacity to recognize a degree of "otherness" was actually essential to his role as a manager.

This was not the same as aloofness or unfriendliness, but his role as a manager included the need to appraise his team members' performance, objectively and fairly, and to take responsibility for their career progression. He could not hold back on providing constructive criticism to his close friends, if needed, just as he could not run the risk of any criticism of other people being seen as unfounded because they were not part of a favored circle.

"Dave, I'm wondering what it means to you to be a manager," I said. "How would you define good management?"

He started thinking about the good managers he'd had in his career, who were role models for him. He mentioned qualities like objectivity, the ability to make hard calls, and the need to coordinate the efforts of a group of people so they felt like a team.

"If I'm a good manager, that means I'm going to have to act differently sometimes than how I usually want to act," he said, the reality of his position slowly dawning on him. "I'm not going to be able to pal around with these guys who are some of my best friends. I'm going to have to tell them sometimes that they're not doing a good job." At this, he made a face as if he had just tasted something sour.

He knew his habits needed to change—not just to mature into his adulthood more fully, but to be the kind of manager he wanted to be, one who was considered fair and inclusive.

Creating healthy boundaries

As a result of his expanded awareness, Dave decided that he needed to make some changes. One of the best antidotes to confluence is creating healthy boundaries. Instead of merging, we become clear with ourselves and the world around us about our separateness. It doesn't mean we can't be in relationships with others, but it means that we don't habitually go along to get along, or make decisions from a need to be liked.

In Dave's case, this meant that he started to step back from his social reliance on his buddies at work. Because they knew he was being coached, I encouraged him to be transparent with them about why he was having lunch with them less frequently, for instance. It was out of his desire to be a better leader, and he wanted to be perceived as being equitable to all.

Dave wanted to maintain his habit of socializing with his team, but he wanted to be more inclusive. Besides cutting back on the frequency of informal meetings with his previous inner circle, he began to systematically meet with every member of the team, making sure that everyone was getting the same amount of access to him.

He spent time getting to know team members, and he guided conversations toward work issues so that he could gauge people's opinions and encourage honest feedback. His team came away with the feeling that they and Dave knew each other a bit better, that they knew what the team had to achieve, and their role in it. The team was pulling together in the same direction.

Several excellent new ideas emerged in the course of the one-on-one and team meetings that Dave initiated, as people felt able to make a contribution. Dave ensured that he followed up on these ideas. A real sense of camaraderie began to emerge. Dave's approach to the whole team became—and was seen to have become—fairer and more evenhanded. The team's productivity measurably improved. There was a real buzz in the air.

My first impression of Dave had been that he was a teenager in a man's body. As his self-awareness improved, he began to grow into a man—and in so doing, he became a better leader.

Interestingly, Dave later told me that he had begun to invest more in friendships outside of work that he had neglected, reducing the need to look for supportive relationships at work.

"You know, I got a drink with an old football friend of mine, Frank, and it was good to see him," he said. "It was also easier to hang out with him because we don't have to talk about work stuff, and I'm not his manager. I'm going to do that more."

As he grew into his leadership role, Dave recognized that it could indeed be lonely at the top—and that this was OK, too.

▶ REFLECTIONS ◀

- How important is it for me to be liked by others? To what degree does this need drive my behavior—at work and in life? Is this OK for me?

- Who would I be without a strong drive to be liked? Could I like myself as much as I want others to like me?

- What unintended consequence could there be at work if I need to be friends with everyone, especially those who report to me?

- What kind of leader do I want to be? What do I want my team to say about me?

▶ PRACTICES ◀

- If you are a manager, track how you spend your time in and outside of work with the people who work for you. In general, it should be equitable across the whole team.

- Be consistent when connecting with people—asking them about their weekends, for example. Keep in mind that how you spend your time is always sending messages, whether you realize it or not.

- Speak about other people as if they are in the room with you. Gossip is never helpful and almost always has the potential to harm.

- If you need to vent or process something, find a trusted peer or advisor or coach to talk with—not the people who report to you.

- Put yourself mentally in the position of your team: What would they want from you? What behaviors would they expect and need? Are you delivering those?

- Try making decisions, especially hard decisions, from a place of fairness. Consider whether your feelings about people and your relationships with them might be affecting your decision-making or judgment.

- Begin to see yourself as more invested in your home and social life than in work. Take yourself to your work rather than trying to define yourself at work.

Chapter 3

I Take Care of Everyone Except Myself

I FIRST MET DANIELLE IN a team-building retreat I conducted with the student affairs office of a local university. A high-energy person full of thoughtful questions and a measured dose of idealism, she brought a naturally positive, grounded presence to her team. During the retreat, she discussed how working with the university was her dream job.

We lost touch over time, so I was pleasantly surprised when Danielle reached out several years later to inquire about receiving some executive coaching.

By the time I met with her again, Danielle, a Korean-American woman now in her mid-thirties, didn't seem like the person I knew from the workshop. Her energy was lower than I remembered. She reported that she often felt tired and less motivated these days.

"I've been passed over for a few promotions, and while I didn't know if I even wanted those jobs, I'm confused about why I wasn't even considered," she said. "I'm beginning to notice that I feel resentful toward the university and its leadership, and I'm wondering if maybe it's time for me to find another job."

Danielle indicated that her work-life balance had also gotten out of whack, and she wanted to pay attention to that as well, given her ongoing fatigue and dampened mood. Finally, she indicated that while she loved being a manager and saw herself as a natural coach for her staff, she felt guilty that perhaps she wasn't doing such a good job of looking after others and wondered whether she just wasn't in the right job anymore.

Resentment and guilt are signs of confluence

One of the unhealthy patterns (or interruptions in contact) I look out for in my work with clients is confluence. Confluence is a way in which we unconsciously merge our needs with the needs of the people in our environment, often guided by the belief that we need to take care of others or that we need to submerge our own needs to feel safe.

When clients report feeling guilt, resentment, or both, I'm particularly clued into the fact that confluence might be afoot, since feeling guilty or resentful are often signs that we are overriding our own needs by attending more to what others need.

As Danielle and I started the coaching process, I asked her to tell me about what she was experiencing and why it felt so difficult. The first thing she told me was that she currently did the work of nearly three people. One colleague had recently been assigned to work on a special project with the university president, and her workload had been transferred to Danielle. Another colleague had an elderly parent that needed care in another state, so she had taken time off, leaving additional work as well. Many new projects had landed on Danielle's plate, and she was trying to keep up.

She wasn't happy about this, but she also didn't complain. It meant that she ended up staying later at the office than she wanted, often missing her favorite yoga class.

"I feel like I need to just suck it up and soldier on to be a good manager," she said.

It never occurred to her to raise her hand and say that it was too much. That wasn't her style.

To make matters more complex, Danielle's own manager had resigned early on in our work together. In what I've seen across many organizations, a not-so-effective leader is sometimes asked to leave, but instead of it being done with some transparency, the shift is done mostly in secret. While this can leave an organization in better standing in the long run, short-term shifts like this can be destabilizing for people inside the organization who don't know what's going on and have to quickly pick up the pieces.

"How do you feel about your manager leaving?" I asked.

"You know, it's complicated," she said and smiled.

"I don't know if you realized it, but you just smiled. What made you smile?"

"She was really a nice person, but if I'm honest, she didn't do her job very well," Danielle said. "She put off a lot of decisions and didn't do a tremendous amount of work. I felt like I actually ended up working more, not less, when she joined our team. There are times when I covered for her in meetings when it became clear she hadn't followed up with something. I'm sad because I liked her, but I'm also relieved because it would be great to have a more competent manager in that job."

"It sounds like you were doing a lot to help her be successful," I said.

"Yeah, a lot."

Without being asked, Danielle had quietly cleaned up the small messes her manager created with other team members. She also stepped in after the manager said things in meetings that contradicted the strategic direction of the university or made decisions that were not based on what the department had learned over time. It was obvious that Danielle overfunctioned for her boss.

Overfunctioning and underfunctioning

A common dynamic I see in organizations is familiar from the world of family dynamics: the role of "overfunctioners" and "underfunctioners" in a system. As the name suggests, overfunctioners tend to act in a way that goes beyond what is actually asked of them. Systems—family or organizational—often get accustomed to the short-term benefits over-functioners provide, because if you let an overfunctioner do her thing, she'll make your life easier by doing things that you might have otherwise done.

Conversely, underfunctioners tend to do less than their share. Sometimes this is out of a lack of drive, ability, or just a habitual pattern. They may want to do more but the overfunctioners in their environment just kick in too quickly. Often, though, there's a benefit inherent for the under-functioner, because by doing less, or standing still, the overfunctioner gets her cue to do more.

They are a system of intertwined parts. I like to bring awareness to the benefits (and drawbacks) of the two roles.

I did this with Danielle, since it was clear that she was an overfunc-tioner in a confluent way of ensuring that everyone else was taken care of and happy, apart from herself. She had never stopped to think about what she was doing. In her mind, a job needed to get done—or in her case, four jobs, including her own—and she felt it was her responsibility to step up and do them.

If only she weren't so tired and unmotivated.

Is the past present?

Danielle and I started looking at her history. I was intrigued by why she took on so much and when this habit had started.

"Is the role of caretaker familiar to you?" I asked. "Taking care of others, making sure they're OK? Not looking out for yourself as much as you do everybody else?"

Danielle looked confused at first, then she seemed to gain some clarity. "That's who I am," she said. "That's what I've been doing all my life."

We both paused. I looked at Danielle and she looked at me. Bright and thoughtful, Danielle had studied education in college. She was having a revelation and knew it, which was just what I was hoping for. She began to smile.

"What makes you smile?" I asked.

"Well, I guess the truth is I am just playing out the role I've had with everyone in my life," she replied. "It's just that now it's happening at work, and I'm realizing I've really been on autopilot."

It's my experience that these kinds of habits, of the mind and heart, are often some combination of nature and nurture, and over time we unconsciously make conclusions about the world and our place in it based on how we've learned to get along.

Danielle had been a caretaker for everyone around her, ever since she could remember. She was the peacemaker when her parents argued—which wasn't often, but with enough regularity that she remembers stepping in to calm them down during a heated moment. She was the diplomat on her sister's behalf, when she did something wrong, and their parents were upset with her.

She was also the caretaker for her many girlfriends over the years. In one friendship, for instance, one young friend felt the need to be "cool" on the exterior at school, but only with Danielle did she allow herself to still play with dolls.

She essentially planned another friend's wedding even though she wasn't asked to do it and wasn't even a bridesmaid. Danielle did it because she sensed it needed to get done, and she had the skills to do it. Her grateful friend still credits Danielle, saying she "made the wedding happen." But Danielle was confused because instead of feeling pleased and flattered, she felt sad and even angry at her friend.

"Does it sound true that you've lived as if you had to take care of everyone else, and you came last on the list?" I asked her.

She nodded enthusiastically. She knew it was true, and it felt good to say it out loud, even it didn't feel good while it was happening.

We also spent some time looking at *why* Danielle might have come to that conclusion. This question is always a little tricky, since we develop our coping mechanisms over time and usually starting from a young age when we're not even conscious of why we are doing what we're doing. For Danielle, though, given her honest approach and her refined self-awareness, she was able to see that she had benefited from being the caretaker. She could also see that being born into a Korean-American family only amplified this belief, since she was raised to believe that women were *supposed* to be the family caretakers.

"I think I acted this way because it was my way of getting attention and approval from my family and friends," she said. "This way of being responsible has always made me important in the eyes of those around me, and I also like the way it feels good to take care of people."

"What's the downside?" I asked.

"Look at me: I'm tired, I feel unmotivated, and I'm really not that happy these days," she said. "This isn't working the way it once did."

We can only change our behavior once we have become deeply aware of what we are habitually doing.

For a while, I just asked Danielle to notice her patterns: how quickly she volunteered to take something on when no one else did; how quickly she stepped in to take care of her boss when she had failed; how quickly she felt guilty when an employee who reported to her felt dissatisfied in her job and wanted Danielle to "fix" it.

What would the black leather jacket do?

As our work progressed, I asked Danielle to start noticing whether she could imagine different ways of responding to her environment instead of her habitual patterns of caretaking.

Danielle looked puzzled. As she struggled to envision what it would be like to show up differently at work, I remarked on the black leather jacket she was wearing and how I hadn't seen her in it before.

In New York City, seeing a person in a black leather jacket is not such a big deal, but Danielle looked different in it. Normally, she dressed in tasteful business casual attire, including traditional sweater sets in cool, calm colors. The black leather jacket was a different statement—rough and edgy. It didn't say "caretaker" to me.

I wondered whether Danielle could let the jacket affect her, too.

"If your leather jacket had a personality, what would it be?"

Danielle laughed. "I don't know. She wouldn't give a shit, really. She would walk into the office and feel confident in her swagger. She would say what was on her mind, and she wouldn't try to clean up everyone's messes."

"Huh, sounds interesting," I said. "Would you be willing to give it a try?"

For the next several weeks, Danielle played with the idea that the black leather jacket could be her guide for how she could show up differently at work. While it seemed like a funny way to find direction, it was usually clear, in most instances, what Danielle in the leather jacket would do.

During this time, Danielle set up a meeting with the university's dean of students, which she had been wanting to do for some time but kept putting off initiating it because she assumed the dean would be too busy. At this meeting, Danielle told the dean that she had been feeling unhappy of late and that she had realized through coaching and self-reflection that she spent too much time taking care of everyone around her. She reported that doing the jobs of her two peers was no longer acceptable, and that a new plan was needed.

She said that she had supported her former boss perhaps more than the dean knew, and it made Danielle realize that she should reassert her interest in a future promotion. She added that she had been in the student affairs office for a significant period of time and felt she should have more of a seat at the table when it came to the bigger strategic decisions affecting the office's direction.

The dean told Danielle she was pleased that Danielle had initiated the meeting. She also told her how valuable she was and even suggested that perhaps there were times that Danielle had been overlooked for higher-level roles with more visibility because she was clearly so good at being in the trenches. The dean became interested in Danielle's ambitions and asked her to schedule a time the following month when they could continue the conversation.

"I've been at the university for four years, and I always assumed that my hard work would pay off, and I would be rewarded," Danielle said. "But I'm realizing I made an assumption that no one was aware of but me. I might have to advocate for myself if I want a promotion."

As our work together progressed, she began to take greater control of her career. Without her previous anger, resentment, and guilt, Danielle felt lighter and reported having more energy. She was getting more rest, too, and the circles under her eyes had gone away.

In Danielle's four years at the university, she had never been so clear about her own needs, and she had not heard the dean take such an interest in her future in quite some time. It was as if the dean had unconsciously gone along with Danielle's habit of putting Danielle's needs last, and it was as if both of them were waking up to another way of doing things.

Showing up differently

By the time our work came to an end, several months later, Danielle was starting to show up differently—in her job and in her life. She was making time to exercise on a regular basis and to attend that yoga class she loved. She was leaving work at 6 p.m., not 8 p.m., and she had worked with colleagues to divvy up the work left by the two peers versus taking it all on herself. She spent a weekend alone, for the first time in years, and organized her closet in ways that she had been putting off for a long time. She looked happier, healthier, and more alive.

"I know it sounds crazy, but I just organized my closet for forty-eight hours, and I am so frickin' happy right now!" she said. "I'm doing my yoga again, listening to music, and dancing in my living room. I'm enjoying myself, and I'm not exhausted at the end of the day."

Meanwhile, Danielle met with the employee of hers, Katrina, who had continually tried to put Danielle in the "driver's seat" of her career development. Danielle looked at Katrina and told her that she needed to take more responsibility for what she wanted from her career. Danielle said she was happy to help and support Katrina, but it was her life to live, and Danielle was no longer going to overfunction for her in this way. Katrina looked surprised but also pleased. Sometimes people actually want to be given boundaries and clarity, and this seemed to be the case for Katrina.

You never want to say "I told you so" to a client, but I was really satisfied.

"It sounds like it's good to remember that we all have to clean up our side of the street. You can't do everything for everyone else, nor can they do everything for you," I said, and Danielle nodded. "She needed to attend to her own work around what she wanted from her career, and now it sounds as if she's willing to take ownership instead of outsourcing it to you. Is that right?"

"Yes!" Danielle said.

"I hear relief in your voice," I said. It was palpable.

She agreed.

"And what's also interesting is that it gives you more opportunity to do that for yourself," I continued. "In a way, there's a parallel process here. Katrina wants to do more of what she loves, and I think you do, too."

"Absolutely," said Danielle, nodding vigorously, her eyes wide and full of excitement.

This news didn't surprise me. Employees want to learn, and they want to grow, and sometimes that can take time, effort, and even frustration. Leaders must find the balance of supporting their employees while also challenging them to work through obstacles.

It doesn't mean, of course, that a leader isn't available for mentoring, coaching, and higher-level support if organizational constraints can be removed. But it actually isn't in the long-term interest of the employee if the leader simply takes care of everything. It's exhausting for the leader, and over time, it deprives the employee of their own growth.

Leading others doesn't mean doing things for them—it means creating the conditions so that others can do things for themselves.

As psychotherapists, we're also taught that helpful therapy is a continual balancing act of support and frustration. You want to support and validate the client's experience while creating moments of reflection and insight for them. Sometimes, that requires frustrating (or challenging) their habitual ways of thinking and behaving.

While being a leader is in many ways different from being a therapist, in this sense I've always seen a parallel. It's not about abandoning one impulse or the other—it's about creating a healthy balance that serves everyone involved.

Danielle is still not sure if she will stay at the university much longer, as it has been nearly five years now, and she is getting clearer about *what she wants* versus what the student affairs office needs from her. In one of our last sessions, we distilled some of her specific strengths when it comes to operations and management, and she realized that there were other places calling to her.

Danielle still wears her black leather jacket sometimes. It's no longer a pointer, though. With time and practice and some natural relapses along the way, Danielle has largely been able to shift out of her habit of chronic caretaking and has reported feeling more balanced. While she's still able to attune to what others need and is appreciated for her empathy, she now possesses a heightened awareness of what it means to take care of herself and to choose her own joy first.

As opportunities arise, Danielle is thinking about taking on something new.

"All this time, I've felt like I needed to make sure everything was running well at work, but I had ended up getting tired, and even a little bored," she said. "I'm so excited by the idea that my next job might be about what I want. I want to do something not because it's the thing that needs to get done, and no one is doing it, but because I enjoy it."

► REFLECTIONS ◄

- Do I habitually take care of others in my personal and/or professional life?

- Do I or others think of my informal role as a "caretaker"?

- What do I get out being a caretaker? What benefit was there to being a caretaker in my family of origin and/or with my friendships growing up?

- What are the costs to me (and others) of my being a habitual caretaker?

- Who would I be if I weren't the caretaker?

- What are my behavioral patterns around caretaking? Are there certain people or situations that trigger me to act in this way?

- Do I feel guilty or resentful with some regularity? (Reminder: These are signs of confluence.)

▶ **PRACTICES** ◀

- Use the feelings of guilt and resentment as useful signposts: When chronically felt, they almost always point us to ways in which we are being confluent with others.

- Practice setting boundaries before you think you should. This is similar to stopping work before you are tired. There is lag time, and you are not practiced in creating boundaries to protect your own time, energy, and well-being.

- Put on your own proverbial "air mask" before you help others with theirs. If you are feeling drained, tired, or ambivalent about offering your help or taking care of others, start by meeting your own needs first—and then see where you land.

- Find a symbol—for Danielle, it was the black leather jacket, but it could be a thing or a person who practices balance well—and ask yourself, "What would they do in this situation?" Lean on wisdom, experience, and temperament that you are still developing.

- Practice saying no more often—at home and at work. You can say it with love and with kindness, but you can still say it. Practice not volunteering for so many things and see how that feels. If you feel agitated, that is natural—practice tolerating your discomfort before doing anything about it.

- Even though it has become a bit of a cliché, practice self-care when you can. Whether that means exercising, resting, socializing, or practicing a hobby, make sure you develop a habit of doing things you enjoy on a regular basis. This is an easy way not to feel resentful of others, because by practicing self-care, you have not deprived yourself of your own pleasure.

▶ **EXPERIMENTS** ◀

- Try small ways of *leaning into caretaking* or *leaning out of caretaking*—but with conscious awareness, not on autopilot. Notice the difference in your energy and mood.

- Share with a person who's important to you what it's like to be a caretaker and discuss what it might be like for you to show up differently in your relationship; share what you might need from your friend to help support you.

- If you're a leader, practice playing with the balance of *being challenging* with *being supportive* of your staff. Find ways to help them "learn to fish" versus "giving them the fish" and see what happens.

Chapter 4

I'm Just Not Good Enough

I FIRST MET BENJAMIN, A high-powered attorney from Washington, DC, shortly after his firm had undergone an acquisition. All of the company's top leaders were given executive coaching to support them through the process, and Benjamin's boss sat in on our first session.

"You're a really smart guy, Ben. You're a great attorney and I trust you implicitly," his boss said. "But you'll finish a great presentation and afterwards, in the hallway, you'll ask me how you did. Like a child. And I get confused. You don't know how you did? You really don't? There's an insecurity there that is startling for me—and it's an issue that I fear could limit your future success."

Benjamin had decades of a successful legal career behind him. A forty-five-year-old white man, he was smart, ambitious, and every inch the corporate lawyer. Always immaculately dressed, always calm, always in control, and a successful triathlete in his spare time. And yet here was this unaccountable self-doubt, which bewildered his boss and communicated to his colleagues that Benjamin was not quite as commanding and confident as he appeared to be, even after years of receiving positive feedback about his ability to present and lead meetings. As we would learn, his experience as a leader was haunted by a deeper, enduring emotional insecurity.

When I spoke to Ben, he said an inner critical voice told him that he simply wasn't good enough, despite appearances to the contrary.

"After a meeting or presentation, I'm full of misgivings," he said. He bit his lip and concern showed on his face. I saw how his boss could perceive him as a child. "I wonder if it was all that good. I remember the look someone gave me and then I think they must be judging me. Then I think, no, I definitely wasn't good. In fact, I was a disaster."

"Does this voice ring any bells?" I asked.

He shrugged and said that, no, it didn't. It had been there as long as he could remember.

My coaching work with Benjamin continued for several weeks, and I came to learn how deeply familiar his inner critic was in his psyche. No matter what he did at work, he often questioned himself afterward and told himself he could have done better. Benjamin could also be critical of others. (In my experience, the two dynamics often, though not always, go hand in hand.)

Recently, his administrative assistant had come to his office crying, feeling as if maybe she should quit. She told Benjamin that she didn't think she was good enough for her job, or for Benjamin. She had come to this conclusion after he gave her some pointed feedback because of an error she made filing a legal brief.

"I don't want to be seen as that dude, that asshole in the office," Benjamin told me. "But I also need for things to be done right."

"Does the voice that criticized your assistant sound like the voice in your head, telling you that you didn't do things well enough?"

"Oh yeah," he smiled. "It's the same voice. I'm not good enough. And frequently, neither is anyone else."

Finding the origins and separating out the voices

As coaching progressed, I asked Benjamin more about his childhood and upbringing. I knew very little about him, and I realized I might have been making assumptions based on outward appearances. I imagined that maybe he was the product of high-achieving parents, a prep school education, or Ivy League conditioning. It turns out I was incorrect.

As I got to know him, and over weeks of discussing how much he was either doubting himself or others at work, we eventually arrived at Benjamin's upbringing—a background I never would have imagined given Benjamin's outward sophistication.

As a young child, he had been physically abused and later abandoned by a mentally ill, drug-addicted mother. After that, he went to live with his father, who didn't have much time for him and gave him little love or attention.

"Very few people know the extent of my childhood history. I don't want them feeling sorry for me, and I don't want to have a 'poor me' attitude, but my childhood was very rough. It was beyond words in many ways," he said, his expression somber. "My mom was abusive. She was usually high on drugs, and by the time I went to live with my dad, he had remarried and was raising my stepsiblings. I know my dad cared, and I'm grateful that he stepped in when he did, but he wasn't affectionate or warm."

The fact that he emerged from childhood as a viable adult was remarkable in itself. That he went on to have a highly successful career and become a great father and husband was doubly so.

As our coaching deepened, I learned that Benjamin's critical voice had been developed in childhood to exert control over himself—to step in with authority for the parents who were unavailable. We all do some form of this, by the way. Early in our lives, most of us develop "creative adjustments," a term from Gestalt psychotherapy. Creative adjustments are coping mechanisms or defenses we develop to adapt to our early circumstances. By definition, they are creative, functional, and reasonable reactions to our early environment. This can be anything from a habit of self-criticism to a habit of taking care of others in relationships.

In and of themselves, creative adjustments are not the problem—but when they become our default mode of being in the world, they become a barrier. The best way to know a behavior is a creative adjustment is when it's chronic—that is, you tend to do it all the time, you do it without thinking about it, and it's anachronistic—you do it even and especially when the circumstances don't warrant that response. In Benjamin's case, his coping mechanism of driving himself hard and being self-critical was appropriate at age seven, but by forty-five, it had long outlived its usefulness. It also lacked nuance, which is another clue that it's coming from a younger part of ourselves.

As you will see in other chapters, this creative adjustment is also an interruption in contact—specifically, this is retroflection in action. Put most simply, retroflection is controlling or attacking ourselves—usually in a way that resembles what others did to us or what we wish we could have done to them. It is usually some form of auto-aggression, where we attempt to manage ourselves to feel emotionally safe.

Retroflection is probably the most common of the forms of interruption in contact that I see among high achievers in the workplace. Why? Because it can seem quite functional, and because it's often associated with that inner drive that many successful people have. The problem is that this impulse often stems from a lack of something within ourselves, and our inner critic preys on fear in its efforts to push us forward.

A hypercritical driving force

High achievers tend to have a lot of superstition around this hypercritical driving force inside of them. Once they uncover it, they tend to credit it for their success. When I asked one client what life would be like without it, she said, "Well, I think I'd be sitting on the couch eating chocolate all day."

The instinct to attack yourself becomes so ingrained, becomes such a part of you that you cannot imagine life without it. You believe that in its absence, you would simply not be yourself.

Being driven certainly does have its place in life. We all need to get things done. But this particular driver pushes from a place of fear and doubt as opposed to trust and self-confidence. Moreover, there is really no choice in the matter for the person. It is an addictive, compulsive behavior. In a way, it's not even that different from alcoholism, but because we tend to look at productivity as such a good thing, we don't question whether the impulse to be productive is its own compulsion—a way to *not feel* other emotions within us, things like sadness, fear, and longing.

Benjamin was not alone. I'll always remember an article I read in a prominent business journal nearly twenty years ago. The authors had spoken with leaders at a Big Five consulting firm, and they asked them about the qualities they most looked for in hiring new junior consultants out of college. The first two qualities—intellectual horsepower and competitiveness—came as no surprise. But it was other thing that took my breath away and speaks to something slightly more sinister. The third quality this firm looked for in candidates was an underlying psychological belief by the person that they were "never good enough." In essence, this firm had admitted that it had learned to take advantage of the psychological pain high achievers experienced. People who believe they're just not enough will work painfully hard to prove to themselves and others that they are, and the consulting firm had learned to exploit this habit through its recruitment criteria!

Now, while this consulting firm has done quite well for itself in terms of profitability, that is not the only measure of success. First, we must look at the effects that a psychological system of "never good enough" can have on ourselves. But there are also enormous implications that this habitual pattern can have on employees when the leader is coming from this kind of consciousness, communicating this mindset to the people around them, all the time.

If leaders wish to lead well, they must look honestly at what messages they communicate to staff in explicit and implicit ways. Even if the leader wants to motivate their team, if they themselves are coming from a place of psychological insecurity, or attack, they will inevitably and unconsciously communicate that mindset to others.

"I just can't make her happy" or "I'm never good enough" are the things I hear from employees of leaders who are themselves beset by feelings of insufficiency. Leaders have a responsibility to look in the mirror and deal with their own self-attack system, because otherwise they will invariably apply that to others. That's just the way this tends to work. (And it's true for parents as well.)

Remember that when we're coming from a place of self-attack, we are in a reactive "Child state." There is little choice in the matter; we're simply trying to survive. But leadership at its best is less about survival and more about helping to create the right conditions for everyone to thrive. Leadership is also at its best when we are coming from an adult consciousness and not from the emotional psyche of a child.

Strengthening the victim inside of us

The antidote to this kind of behavior begins with shoring up the voice and power of the victim within our psyche—essentially an underdeveloped part of ourselves. Just as you would help an abused person to stand up to a bully, we must learn to support and encourage that part of ourselves that has been victimized and beaten down. At the beginning, this voice almost always tends to be meek and quiescent. It says to the critical voice, "You're right, I'm not enough. Thank you for being here. I'd be nothing without you."

By my pointing out that this dynamic is no longer working and by coaching that faint voice, clients can arrive at a point where they can finally speak up against the inner critic: "It's not helping me when you give me a hard time. I'm still learning this job. I'm smart and I'm trying to figure this out, and I need your support, not your attack."

I'll often encourage a client to visualize the younger part of themselves, the one who developed this coping mechanism in the first place. This was especially potent for Benjamin. When he saw how he was attacking his inner child, he realized the extent of the loss he had suffered when he was young.

We worked together one day over videoconference because he wasn't able to come to my office. I sensed it was a good time to try the empty chair technique to help him connect with the younger part of himself that still needed some support and attention. Benjamin set up an empty chair in his room and sat in another chair a few feet away.

"Imagine yourself as a seven-year-old boy," I began.

He took a moment, and he appeared to choke up a little bit.

"He's a really cute kid. He's really smart. He's been through a lot," Benjamin said softly. "And he's really on his own in the world."

"How does that affect you?"

"It makes me sad. Makes me feel very tenderly toward him."

I continued, "Can you imagine what your dad would say to little Benjamin at a soccer game when he wanted him to know how well he did? Could you offer that to little you?"

He looked at me and shook his head.

"No one ever came to any of my soccer games," he said. He began to tear up again, and his tone was somber. He was slowing down.

I encouraged him to support this inner victim, but the problem he encountered here was that he had no memory of being supported to draw on. There was nothing in his history to provide a template for how you would help and guide someone who needed it, so instead I gently turned us toward his present life.

"I see, so you don't have a model from when you were a kid. And there may be some legitimate grief you feel about that. At the same time, I know you're a great dad yourself with two kids, a boy and girl of your own," I said. "I wonder if you could talk to little Benjamin the way you would talk to your son after a soccer game?"

He began to cry.

"You did such a good job out there. I love you so much, no matter what you do," he said. Tears were streaming down his face, and I had to choke back my own. "I'm so proud of you. I can see how hard you're trying."

In this way, the future can sometimes miraculously heal the past. With practice, Benjamin could use this same voice, the one he used as a dad, to develop a loving and nurturing conversation with the child part of himself.

I said, "Let's invoke the parent you never had. What would that parent say to Benjamin about how he's doing at work?"

Benjamin paused and teared up again. He was deeply moved and could not speak right away. After taking a few deep breaths, he looked across the room, imagining his inner child, and said quietly, "I love you, you're safe. Look how hard you worked to get here. You did a great job in that presentation and I am so proud of you."

In his work, Benjamin came to realize that he had developed his over-functioning critic because he had such little parental supervision growing up. In the absence of a supporting voice, he had developed an inner task-master to ensure that he rose out of the life in which he had been raised, to ensure that he would be hard-working and successful.

Slowly, over time, he practiced replacing his inner critical voice with a nurturing, caring voice, one that had the capacity to motivate through love and understanding rather than intimidation.

Key to the success of this approach was Benjamin's willingness to be vulnerable with me, to open himself up to a kind of conversation that he had never had before. This is not easy to do, but taking this step opens up new emotional possibilities like nothing else.

Freedom from inner attack creates new possibilities

Eventually, Benjamin saw that there was ample life force in the part of himself that he had been trying to stifle and control. His success, it turned out, was not contingent on endless self-harassment, and he learned to use his imagination to draw on the love and care that he showed his own children as a grown man. He became his own loving parent.

As a leader, he grew in self-confidence. Benjamin could bring a high-stakes meeting to a successful conclusion, breathe, feel his feet on the ground, and give himself the reassurance he had previously sought from others. He stopped asking for feedback and started making choices based on what he wanted, not on pleasing the parents he never had. He also approached feedback more gently with the people that worked for him. He came to realize that not only did he not want to attack himself, he didn't want to attack anyone else, either.

"I don't feel the need to ask my boss anymore what he thinks of me because I have a better sense than ever that I'm doing a good job, and I'm proud of that. I also don't want to perpetuate the pain I've endured by being so critical of others," he told me. "Being the father that I wish my dad had been is teaching me something, too, about taking good care not only of my son, but also of myself as an adult."

► REFLECTIONS ◄

- If I'm feeling bad about myself, what's the story that I am telling myself? Which voice am I hearing right now? Could I give it a name or a face to bookmark who it is as a separate part of me? What is that part saying to me?

- How do I feel when I take these thoughts as truth?

- Who is listening to the thoughts? Who is the receiver? Is it a Child state? What age do I think it is?

- What could I say to myself that would be supportive right now?

- If I were speaking to a younger version of myself, or to a child, what would I say? What would I say if I were speaking from a place of love, acceptance, and care?

► PRACTICES ◄

- Practice not just reacting to your negative self-talk, but pausing enough to discern and to listen to what that self-talk is saying. When you hear a negative voice in your head, work to replace it with words that feel more supportive to you. If it's hard for you to do this, imagine the most loving person in your life—real or imagined—saying affectionate and supportive things to you. What would they say? Don't rush through this. Feel how you are affected by these words. Do this as regularly as you can.

- Practice self-care and do things to create ease and relaxation for yourself. Some of us are just not practiced at feeling relaxed. Consider these ideas: Get a massage, take a hike, enjoy a nice meal. Remind yourself what joy, fun, and relaxation feel like.

► **EXPERIMENTS** ◄

- Take time bringing to mind your inner child and get to know them. Spend a couple hours with that part of yourself. A fun thing to do is ask them, "What would be fun to do this afternoon?" Spend a few hours doing that and see what it's like.

- Find a photograph of yourself as a child. Put the picture in a spot where you can see it on a regular basis. Experiment with what it feels like to look at your inner child with love and care, from the place of your inner adult.

Chapter 5

I Know I Should
Address This Conflict, but I Don't

FROM THE MOMENT I MET Amanda, I liked her. She was naturally warm, kind, and friendly, making it easy to be around her—and I wasn't alone in feeling this way. Amanda had a lovely smile and a positive, sincere demeanor that made her a natural "mom" in her consumer products company. People wanted to be around her, to tell her things, to confide in her, and to work with her to make things better within the company.

Amanda's work in Human Resources came easily to her, since she truly cared about people's development. She took her responsibility seriously to support the professional growth of employees. She was known as a great builder of teams, and throughout the years she spent in her company, she had created several happy, productive teams that she managed with great attention and care. Even people who weren't so sure of what HR did wanted to be part of Amanda's team since she created such a positive energy around her.

In reality, then, there was little that created a problem for Amanda, with the exception of situations or people that made her uncomfortable. When she came for coaching, as a high-potential leader in her early forties, Amanda indicated that she wanted to work on her lifelong habit around avoiding conflict. This pattern had shown up many times before, and it now appeared around two specific people in Amanda's work life—Roxanne, a direct report, and Maria, a peer. Both situations made Amanda deeply uncomfortable and she wasn't sure what to do.

"My relationships at work are so good, I feed off of the positivity," she said. "I love my team and the people I work with. These more fraught dynamics are new to me, and they're starting to really stress me out because what I'm doing isn't working."

The direct report—a "gossip machine"

Amanda had not hired Roxanne herself and she probably wouldn't have, given Roxanne's hard personality edges and her reputation as a "gossip machine" in the organization. Instead, Amanda had inherited her as a manager through a recent restructuring.

Where Amanda was naturally positive, Roxanne was negative: She had a snarky way of communicating, putting people down slightly when she talked about them, which was often. Roxanne seemed to build relationships based on loyalty and fear; it was as if she looked to build allies on the team whom she could influence and control. She could make a good meeting turn bad through her offhand remarks about the unfeasibility of a goal; she could make a productive project go off the rails by subverting team efforts if she disagreed. Most of the team members, including Amanda, were intimidated by Roxanne and generally tried to avoid her whenever they could.

In just a couple of months, Amanda had become deeply concerned.

"I don't know what to do about Roxanne. She is wreaking havoc on this team after I worked so hard to create a good dynamic," Amanda said. "I can see that her presence is creating problems that didn't exist before, and I don't want to deal with it because she's really tough. To be honest, I'm a little intimidated by her, too."

Her peer—a well-intentioned but overwhelmed friend

The other person that Amanda was struggling with was Maria. They considered themselves friends after many years of working together in HR in different parts of the country. They shared a deep interest in developing employees and helping people grow. Maria worked in another HR department, but the two women were peers, at the same level of the organization, doing complementary work around employee development.

All was easy in their relationship until Maria and Amanda were asked to co-lead a working group together. Given some changes underway in their company, the two women were asked to manage a companywide project around developing a curriculum for new skills that employees would need to learn related to a shift in company strategy.

Things started off well—Amanda and Maria met for a kick-off meeting of their entire working group, which included a handful of junior staff helping them with the project.

"We left that meeting feeling optimistic about what was possible," Amanda said. "I felt like we were philosophically aligned around what we were setting out to accomplish, and we even scoped out a project plan together. I thought we'd make a good team."

Unfortunately, the project did not continue so positively or easily. Maria got very busy with other, competing demands on her time, especially given a few high-profile projects she had to manage with senior executives closely involved. Over several weeks, Maria slowly did less and less of the work that she had promised to do, and deadlines were starting to be missed.

At first, Amanda just kicked into her normal coping style—she over-functioned, essentially doing her own role and Maria's, too. She figured that Maria would quickly realize that this was not good and that she would kick back into gear. Not so. It seemed that with time, and either out of her own busyness or in the comfort that she had with Amanda doing both jobs, Maria did even less as Amanda did more. She answered fewer emails related to the project, she relied on Amanda to lead the project calls, and she often canceled at the last moment after she had committed to participate in a meeting. Overall, Maria's presence in the group was noticeably absent, so much so that one of the junior staff asked Amanda if Maria was still co-leading the project.

"I just don't know what to do right now about this. Maria is a close friend of mine at work, and we've worked on so many projects together in such a collaborative way," Amanda told me, clearly distressed. "I really care about Maria, but I'm not sure how to bring this up without making her mad. She's just not doing her part."

Unlike Roxanne, who intimidated and even repelled her, it was her close relationship with Maria that made this situation more complex and thornier. Because Amanda didn't want to make Maria angry or defensive, she simply tolerated the situation through clenched teeth and a forced smile.

Looking at our habits

Our coaching work began when Amanda and I started to explore her habits around conflict and how they had formed. Growing up in an Irish-American household with a demanding father, Amanda could easily recognize that throughout most of her life her habit had been to avoid conflict whenever possible, whether it was with her parents, a friend, or a coworker.

"That's the way I've always preserved relationships, and until now, it seems to have worked," she said.

It didn't take long, though, to explore that there was a downside to all of her "conflict avoidance," a habitual behavior that involves avoiding open conflict or disagreement with others. Amanda could recognize that while she was busy looking out for everyone else's interests and making sure they were not mad or upset, she was simultaneously neglecting her own needs.

This often left Amanda with a host of feelings that were uncomfortable—feelings like anger, annoyance, frustration, resentment, and fatigue. It also meant that instead of dealing with difficult situations or people, Amanda found creative ways to avoid the problem, but in so doing she often made more work for herself.

A meeting could take twice as long because she ended up dealing with Roxanne's passive aggression, overt protests, and other forms of resistance. It also meant that more of her time was taken by mediating issues others on the team had with Roxanne instead of telling Roxanne that her behavior was unacceptable. And with Maria, Amanda ended up doing twice as much work in an attempt to preserve their friendship and collegial relationship.

Amanda could see that this habit was not serving her and that she was inadvertently sending negative messages to other members of her team.

"I don't want to create a culture where other people on my team also avoid difficult conversations. That's no good," she said. "It's a habit I actually want to help them learn to break."

She could see that change was needed, but she didn't know how to start.

Understanding the origins of our habits

One of the things I'm usually drawn to when I begin my coaching work with someone who is conflict avoidant is to understand their historical relationship to conflict. Human beings don't really start out being conflict avoidant; think about a baby who cries because she's hungry—there's no avoidance there. The reality is that most of us learn how conflict can be handled through our upbringing and our family patterns.

It did not take long for Amanda to recognize the source of her discomfort with disagreement or difference. The daughter of a demanding, controlling, and unpredictable father who bordered on abusive, Amanda had learned early on to stay "small" and to be as compliant as possible so as to avoid the ire of her dad. The few times she could recall standing up to him were met with his anger, so she astutely concluded to avoid conflict as a way to stay safe, physically and emotionally.

I put out some feelers to see if Amanda might be comfortable discussing her father with me. She seemed open to it.

"It sounds like this is sensitive material, and I really respect that what you're sharing with me suggests there is some trauma related to growing up with your dad," I said. "Do you mind telling me a little bit more?"

"He was unpredictable and uncontrollable at times," she said. I noticed she was nervously tapping her foot. "When I was four years old, he told me to take my tricycle down a set of stars and laughed when I fell. He was mean-spirited, and I knew I shouldn't cross him. It was very clear if I did, he would become physical or scream at me or my mom. I didn't feel safe."

Conflict avoidance became Amanda's coping mechanism, and it made all the sense in the world. The thing is, though, our coping mechanisms make sense until they don't anymore. If only we could stop doing the thing that we do to protect ourselves at the point when it's no longer necessary, but that's not really how things work.

Conflict avoidance was Amanda's creative adjustment. It was her way of dealing with the world around her as a child, but practiced over time, this way of being became chronic, habitual, and anachronistic. Amanda avoided conflicts without being aware that she was even doing it, and she did it regularly whether she was in a threatening situation or not. Her behavior implied that every conflict had the potential to harm her, and so she defended against the possibility of that no matter what.

In the language of the Gestalt interruptions in contact, Amanda was acting in a way that was confluent with her environment, and she regularly deflected even the remotest possibility of a disagreement for fear that it would turn into something bigger.

Keep in mind that you wouldn't have had to experience Amanda's upbringing to be a conflict avoider. In fact, in my experience, it is one of the most common patterns I see in the workplace—disproportionately among women, who were often socialized in a way to suggest their likability would be compromised if they disagreed with others. My observation is that families that are neglectful and abusive, high in conflict behavior, or particularly low in conflict behavior can all be potential breeding grounds for conflict avoidance.

Feedback is supported by good tools

With support, Amanda started to explore how she could show up in new and different ways with Roxanne and Maria. They were excellent opportunities for practice, in distinct relationships.

To support this effort, Amanda and I role-played different conversations in advance, and we tested how these experiences felt for her. We started with Maria, since that relationship was a strong one, and Amanda suspected that even though she was scared of the outcome, she also thought there was a possibility that Maria would be open to what she had to say.

"How does it feel to be having this conversation with me as Maria?" I asked, trying to start slowly and bring her attention first to an awareness of what was happening in her body.

"I have a knot in my stomach," she replied. "I'm breathing more quickly. My heart is fluttering."

I wanted her to know that she was scared and to bring her awareness to that fear, which is an outside reaction to something inside us. There's a motto I find useful to think about in situations like these: "Feel the fear and do it anyway."

"OK, great," I said. "We can slow down here. I invite you to take some nice deep breaths. Notice how that affects you. Feel the ground beneath your feet."

As we practiced the conversation, I asked Amanda to continue staying in touch with her physical sensations and feelings. I also gave her some straightforward feedback tools to use.

It's my experience that when we get emotionally provoked when old pain or fear emerges, we need to identify our feeling as soon as possible, so that we don't act out of old patterns but can make more choices from a place of awareness. If we're participating in a difficult conversation, we also benefit from having a few feedback tools available to us to remind us how to have the conversation in a healthy, clear, and honest place.

To this point, I draw upon a few sources, including a nonviolent communications model created by American psychologist Marshall Rosenberg and the "clearing model" developed by the Conscious Leadership Group. In a nutshell, when we give feedback, we want to do these key things:

- Start by sharing our present-moment experience of what it's like to give feedback and state our intention for the conversation. (The Conscious Leadership Group refers to this as our "first truth.")

- Communicate our feedback to the other person as neutrally as possible, by using observations and not characterizations or interpretations of their behavior.

- Describe the impact of their behavior on us and share our feelings.

- Describe our relationship needs or values.

- Make a request for moving forward—what are we asking the other person to do or not do?

While Amanda was familiar with giving feedback, this was not a mental exercise for her; it was an emotional process that was deeply frightening and disturbing. It's pretty fair to say that she was in a younger emotional state around conflict, so having these tools by her side was critical, but she also needed to learn to tolerate the agitation and panic she felt in her body at the prospect of having the conversation.

"Maria, I want to talk to you about something, and I'm aware I'm a little nervous to tell you this," she began as we role-played in my office. "I care so much about our working relationship that I want to take the time and talk to you."

Amanda took a breath, resettled herself in her chair and sat up.

"Of course," I said, trying to conjure Maria with a little smile and tilt of my head, encouraging her to go on.

This was Amanda sharing her first truth—something we often skip over. But it can help ground us in our own truth, and it can help the other person know where we are coming from.

"As you know, we were asked to co-lead this global project," she continued. "I was so excited to do it with you. We've had so many great collaborations in the past. But to be honest, I'm disappointed and confused. In the last several weeks, I notice you're not responding to emails or following up with next steps."

Amanda paused, and I didn't say anything.

She continued, "The way this is affecting me is that it's making me frustrated and feeling like my team and I have to pull extra weight to make up for what you're not doing. I don't want to feel that way, and because I value our relationship, I need to find out if you still want to work on this. If so, I need you to recommit. And if not, we need to figure out some new roles and responsibilities."

We practiced a few times, and like anything, with repetition Amanda noticed that the experience became more comfortable for her and flowed more easily. While the first few times she delivered the feedback to me as Maria, she used more disclaimers and her voice was soft, indirect, and vague, she eventually became clearer and stronger in what she wanted to say. I also reminded her that candor does not need to cancel out warmth, and that the best communications, in my experience, are done with truth *and* care.

Taking the first step

Amanda asked Maria if she could speak to her soon after our session. The two women met on videoconference for more than an hour, and during that call, Amanda told Maria that she valued their friendship and professional relationship deeply. She said she wanted to strengthen their collaboration by sharing a few things with Maria to support their relationship.

She told Maria that the fact that Maria had increasingly missed attending meetings and calls and didn't respond to emails was creating stress for Amanda and the team. She asked Maria if she could still realistically perform the co-lead role, and if so, she asked Maria to reengage and step back in more. She also requested that Maria respond to emails within forty-eight hours so as not to create backlog on the project.

Maria responded with openness and grace to the feedback that Amanda shared. (As you might imagine, Amanda was deeply relieved.) Maria quickly recognized the truth in what Amanda was saying. Instead of getting defensive, she took responsibility for the fact that she had, indeed, stepped back from her agreements. She could see that by doing this without saying anything, she had left Amanda holding the bag, and she felt regret because it was unintended. She agreed that she needed to be more realistic about whether she could still be in the co-lead role with Amanda, and instead of making the decision immediately, she asked Amanda if they could try for a few weeks to see how things went with her renewed commitments, and then they would go from there.

Amanda came to our next session with an enormous smile on her face. She felt excited by the idea that she had initiated a difficult conversation with a close colleague and that it had gone as well as it did. She also felt proud that she had spoken truthfully to Maria and that she had not delivered one of the more watered-down messages that she had first practiced out of fear.

"I couldn't believe it," she said. "I was so nervous before the call but after practicing with you, I felt like I had my words and I could see that she was open to what I had to say. She wasn't defensive, and it was a great conversation."

"That's terrific, Amanda," I said. "How did you feel afterwards?"

She didn't miss a beat, saying, "I felt clear and I felt strong."

Amanda felt hopeful, too, that whether Maria stayed in the co-lead role with her or not, it was going to be OK. They now had a more honest exchange that would hopefully enable them to have a real discussion about whether things were working or not.

Working your way up

That left Roxanne and a conversation Amanda was even more scared about, and perhaps with more reason. The truth was that Roxanne could be openly defensive, salty, and defiant. She could say things in a flip way that left other people hurt. She would likely get defensive, and Amanda feared how she would handle this.

We started by practicing a new role-play—mentally putting Roxanne in the empty chair, so Amanda could also see how many projections she had about Roxanne. (Again, our projections are usually what we fear or hope others think.) The fact that we are projecting does not mean we are always inaccurate, but we do have to learn to recognize how much of what we feel comes from our own imagination and fear. Amanda imagined that Roxanne would get angry with her, and she found herself freezing as a result.

I asked Amanda if this reminded her of anything, and her eyes welled up with tears. She could see how deeply ingrained her fear of conflict was, related to her father who had indeed been unpredictable and occasionally violent. To draw from neuroscience, the amygdala, the part of our brain that registers fear, usually give us three options, primitive in nature, when we feel threatened—fight, flight, or freeze. Amanda was used to freezing.

I reminded Amanda to breathe. I also suggested that while all of this had been true in the past, it was no longer true. I invoked the "Parent-Adult-Child (PAC)" model from "Transactional Analysis," a psychoanalytic theory that looks at our state of consciousness (Parent, Child, or Adult) as a basis for understanding behavior. (For more about the PAC model in action, see Chapter 11).

"When you're feeling this way, you're in a Child state," I explained. "There's nothing wrong with our inner child, but she generally doesn't make a strong leader of other adults. Let's bring your inner adult into the room, not to replace, but to accompany your scared child. What would your most loving inner adult say to little Amanda?"

"I've got this," Amanda replied. "You don't need to do this alone. Just stay by my side while we speak to Roxanne."

As she spoke, she visibly relaxed and moved her shoulders down and back, the way you might do in a yoga class. She stretched out her arms above her head, like a sun salutation, and exhaled.

She had the support that she needed and started to realize that she could now find it within herself.

A manager's job is to manage others

When she was in Adult consciousness, I could also remind Amanda of another important and relevant fact: *She was Roxanne's boss.*

I met a seasoned female executive years ago who told me what she had ultimately concluded about being a good leader. "Leadership is not about being liked; it's about being respected. And the dirty little secret about being respected is that people usually like you too."

Some of us avoid conflict to be liked. Others, like Amanda, do it because we want to feel emotionally safe. Whatever the reason, we limit our effectiveness and influence as leaders by constantly avoiding conflict. Over time, leaders like this also lose respect and influence.

There are many hard things about leadership. This includes holding people accountable for doing their jobs and meeting their goals, reprimanding staff if they've caused a problem, and fostering open conversation and decision-making. These are simply some of the truths of leadership, and if we want to lead, we have to be willing to learn to tolerate and eventually become more comfortable with disagreement or conflict.

To do that, we must look at the early messages and conditioning we had regarding conflict and build our conflict management muscle. Like anything, what is awkward at first gets easier with practice. As we get used to it, we help others at work see that conflict is simply a part of life, and that good leadership creates the conditions for healthy conflict to occur.

Given Amanda's role in the organization, she had the authority to reprimand Roxanne, to promote her, and to make decisions about her compensation. By cowering from this positional power, due to her fear and avoidant patterns, Amanda instead had been acting like *she worked for Roxanne* when it was actually the other way around.

Amanda nodded slowly when I reminded her of the reality of their roles.

Once I've built some trust with a client, I feel ready to give them some more direct feedback about what I've witnessed. I was at that point with Amanda now.

"What I'm confused about is that you're *the boss*, and Roxanne works *for you*," I said, speaking slowly on purpose so I could get through to the part of her brain that had been hijacked by fear. "The fact that she works for you means that you can tell Roxanne when she's not behaving well. You can reprimand her when she's being insubordinate or disrespectful toward you or other people. You can decide whether she works for the company or not, in fact, because you have that power. I'm not saying you should use it without thinking it through, but I want to remind you what a manager is and the positional power you have. Does that make sense to you?"

"Yeah," she said, sounding surprised. "A lot of sense."

"That's your job here," I said. "The other thing that's important to understand is that if you don't do your job as manager, you send a signal to the other members of the team that you're not going to take care of them, inadvertently undermining a sense of trust for everyone. This starts having an effect on others, see what I mean?"

"Oh, yes. I can see that."

That was the clincher. The last thing Amanda would ever want to do would be to hurt other people, and we had finally found an intellectual and emotional hook for change to happen. Now she could tell herself, *I don't want to hurt or neglect other people—and it's my job to make sure that doesn't happen.*

We went over a manager's job again to reinforce that it was her role to reprimand an employee if they did something unacceptable or if they were having a negative effect on the team.

Roxanne had been doing both for some time. Amanda's eyes widened when she realized that out of her old habits, she was actually neglecting other members of the team and not protecting them from Roxanne's negativity and gossip. This was motivating for her, and as a result she felt even clearer about the need to speak to Roxanne, since it was in keeping with her values around team health and cohesion, as well as her wish to cultivate "psychological safety" for the people around her. Psychological safety creates a sense of emotional security that gives rise to better morale, productivity, and creativity in the workplace.

"You know, I was willing to put off these conversations, especially the one with Roxanne because she can be such a pain," Amanda said. "But once we put it into the context of being a good manager and a good leader, I saw something differently. It's like it was the push I needed."

After practicing a few times throughout one coaching session, Amanda indicated that she felt ready. Still scared, but ready. This is something else that's critical to understand about ourselves, especially when we change old emotional habits: We should not expect ourselves to never feel scared anymore—especially when we are trying a brand-new behavior that goes against everything we learned to feel safe in the world.

As vulnerability expert Brené Brown suggests, courage is not the absence of fear but our willingness to act despite our fear.

Prepare to be surprised

In our next session, Amanda started out by saying that the conversation with Roxanne was both harder and easier than she had imagined. Harder because while Roxanne initially became defensive, she soon cried after Amanda delivered her feedback to her. It was clear that Roxanne did not like being reprimanded or put on "warning" in her job. She could see that she had been acting in a destructive and defiant way, and she revealed to Amanda that she was going through a separation from her husband. She had been dealing with tremendous stress outside of work that made it tempting to bring conflict into the workplace too.

At the same time, the conversation was also easier than Amanda expected. Instead of fighting with Roxanne, Amanda realized she could simply step into her own power, her own role as manager, to do the right thing. Having coached managers internally to have difficult performance conversations, Amanda was now doing it herself, and she was reminded that this, too, was part of her job.

"As hard as it was at first, it felt good that I could speak truthfully and that I could draw a clear line with Roxanne after all this time," she said.

They laid out a plan for next steps, and Amanda made clear to Roxanne that she would be holding her accountable for changes in her attitude and behavior that would need to be made.

Things progressed well after that for Amanda. She and Maria were able to work out their co-leadership for another month, and eventually Maria asked another person to step in for her since she could see that she could not realistically manage as hoped. Amanda was happy about this, because what she wanted most was to preserve her working relationship with Maria and to not burn out doing two jobs.

Roxanne eventually left the company, mostly because of her divorce and so that she could move closer to her family. But the good news is that this happened after a positive turnaround of her behavior based on discussions with Amanda. Roxanne was able to get some outside coaching, and she realized that for a long time she had been creating workplace dramas and spreading gossip as a way to avoid her own pain at home. She took more responsibility for her habitual negativity and started to act more positively and kindly toward members of the team. She no longer created factions on the team, and she was able to slowly establish herself as someone who wanted to make things better, not worse. She credited Amanda for her "wake-up call" and when she left, it was on good terms.

Amanda grew too, in more ways than one. Not only did she step more into her power as a leader, but her voice grew stronger in other settings when she disagreed and felt something important was at stake. She no longer cowered in the face of strong colleagues, and she shared later with me that this also affected her marriage.

Amanda had habitually avoided conflict with her husband, but after her coaching experience and the shifts she had made, she no longer felt inclined to be avoidant with him. While at first this shift startled her husband, who wasn't used to Amanda telling him she disagreed with him, with time they were able to find a new equilibrium. He appreciated feeling her strength and clarity, and Amanda reported feeling even more satisfied in her marriage, since she was expressing her emotional honesty more regularly.

She also brought more of her authentic self to the workplace, replacing her business suits with more stylish and comfortable clothes, decorating her office with plants and chimes, and sitting on a yoga ball instead of a traditional chair. It became clear to her that by squashing one piece of herself, she had also squashed other parts, and now she was able to show up more fully.

"My lifelong habit has been to avoid conflict, and I'm just realizing how much energy it took to do that," she said. "I feel energetic and alive. And I feel more like, well, myself."

- What did I learn implicitly or explicitly from my family about conflict?

- What were the messages I picked up on or heard about conflict?

- What is my typical conflict behavior (e.g., avoidant, compliant, aggressive)?

- How is my behavior helping me get what I need or not?

- What beliefs do I have about conflict?

- What fears do I have about conflict?

- Do I feel equipped with adequate tools to deal with conflict or disagreement?

▶   PRACTICES   ◀

- Try to articulate for yourself: *What is the story I'm telling myself about having this conversation? If I do it, what do I think will happen? How likely is that?*

- If you're a manager or leader, practice what it's like to express yourself as directly as possible without disclaimers, caveats, or indirectness.

- Find an accountability partner at work to help remind you of your intentions and to practice with when you need the support.

- Use feedback tools like the ones described in this chapter to support you in speaking truthfully and thoughtfully in a way that will get you closer to what you want.

▶   **EXPERIMENTS**   ◀

- Start small: Instead of bringing up the biggest problem with the most difficult person in your life, talk to someone you trust about something minor that you wish were different.

- Experiment with having a difficult conversation through role-playing with a coach or a friend or by using the "empty chair" (usually best done with a witness).

  - Notice how you may change your communication style when you're uncomfortable.

  - Notice in your body any shifts, sensations, or energy when you're practicing the difficult conversation or even imagining it.

Chapter 6

I Don't Want to Play Politics

TRAVIS STARTED WORKING AT A venture capital firm straight out of business school. He wanted to move back to New York from Chicago after graduating, partly to live closer to his family. He was also extremely motivated by entrepreneurial energy. Funding startup firms bursting with innovation and top talent was a way to be "close to the action," and Travis felt inspired by this possibility.

The first several months at the firm were exhilarating for Travis. He learned a tremendous amount about early-cycle investing and the due diligence required to assess whether an investment was a good bet or not. He also learned that while startup entrepreneurs were often excellent salespeople, they weren't always rigorous or realistic about the financial projections they provided to Travis and his firm.

One of the trickiest parts of Travis's job was not taking people at face value, especially around how confident they felt about their company's growth potential. Over time, he learned to ask the right questions to get a comprehensive and realistic look at how a company was growing financially, so his firm could make the soundest investments possible.

That was just the client-facing part. But there was another, potentially more treacherous, part of his job, and that was working with the two cofounders and principals of the firm. Not only did Travis, a twenty-seven-year-old African-American man, have to navigate a predominantly white workplace, but he also had to deal with particularly complicated office politics.

One of the firm's principals, George, a white man in his mid-fifties, was even-tempered and kind, if not a little aloof. George was not around the office much, but when he was, he provided the coaching and guidance that Travis was seeking when he joined.

Alan, the other partner, also white, was as loud and boisterous as George was taciturn. Alan was in his early forties and was also a successful entrepreneur, having grown several companies from startup to publicly traded. In contrast to George, Alan had a brash and aggressive way of expressing himself, given two successful decades of working in venture capital.

You knew when Alan was in the room. You knew as soon as he joined a call by way of his booming voice and his assertive style. Alan had a lot to say and he assumed people wanted to hear it. Alan also did not take lightly to criticism, especially when it was done publicly—or worse, by someone junior to him.

Travis quickly realized that to be successful at his firm, he needed to access George as a mentor and exercise caution around Alan, who was more unpredictable and even volatile when upset. Walking that line, especially as a young man of color, was more difficult than he imagined.

The difficulties begin

Travis told me about two situations he had faced with Alan just a few weeks before we first met.

Travis had been busy for months working on a deal with a startup out of Seattle that was pitching itself as a twenty-first century online clothing store for Millennials. He thought their business model, based on sustainability, was sound and exciting. Half of the garments they sold were gently used, and the other half were manufactured by fair trade producers.

Travis had concluded, based on months of due diligence, that the startup was worth the investment and he was excited that his first big deal was about to go through. On one of the final internal meetings before making the financial transfer, Alan got on the phone.

He picked apart Travis's financial analysis and projections, and he criticized Travis for some questions that he had not asked going into the decision-making round. Alan also caught the fact that some critical data was still missing from the pitch package, and he berated Travis for not having completed this step.

While Travis felt all of Alan's points were valid, he was hurt and embarrassed by being spoken to in such a disrespectful way. He also felt frustrated that Alan had not been available to help support Travis through his first deal, despite repeated requests.

"He's just not interested in mentoring me, or anyone else, for that matter," Travis told me.

If Alan had coached him, any errors could have been remedied before the final meeting, yet Travis bit his tongue. If he had been honest, he would have said that Alan, as his manager, was equally responsible for the errors due to his lack of oversight and support.

But raising that issue, Travis said, "wouldn't be a good idea."

Just a week later, in another meeting, Travis was faced with an equally difficult choice. The team was discussing another firm that they were considering investing in. This was a personal fitness startup, cofounded by an old friend of Alan's. Alan seemed smitten with the investment from the start. His enthusiasm for the startup's potential was obvious. He spoke glowingly about a future dominated by their unique approach to the fitness industry.

Travis didn't see it quite this way. Understanding the needs of his fellow Millennial consumers, Travis actually felt the fitness firm was missing the mark in some ways. He did not feel the investment was such an obvious win, and he wondered whether Alan's judgment was clouded by his friendship with the cofounder. Travis took a chance during the meeting and expressed his views.

"I wonder whether we are missing something here," he said. "It seems like they're only giving us growth projections based on their own internal market research, and they've left out a list of potential threats from the competition. I'm seeing home-based virtual fitness products accelerating, and that could make a fitness studio way less relevant in the future."

Alan glared in Travis's direction. Everyone around the table was quiet. It was clear that Travis had done the thing most were scared to do: He had expressed a difference of opinion to Alan, and there was a collective anticipation of the fall out.

"You're wrong," Alan said.

And that was that.

"I thought this might be what people mean when they say you have to 'play politics' to be successful," Travis told me.

Playing politics and losing sleep

In my work as a coach, I probably hear something about "playing politics" or the need to "be political" on a weekly basis from clients navigating organizational life. I've concluded that there's something about people working together, especially when power is in the mix, that often gives rise to one's perception of "politics" at hand.

I always get curious when I hear the word come up, because while I know that politics is a real thing, I'm also aware that when we say "politics" we may be talking about a whole host of different, but related, dynamics at play. I encourage my clients to understand and specify *the actual dynamics* that are happening versus creating too much of a generalization. By being specific about what is happening, we can get clearer about what choices we feel are available to us, and we can also explore the trade-offs we may have to make.

While there are many dimensions to politics in an organization, two of the dynamics I see most often were true in Travis's situation: 1) a subtle or overt pressure to support someone in their "deal" or in a decision so that they support you in the future around something you care about, and 2) a reluctance to speak truthfully to powerful people at work, especially if the truth is perceived as critical to the person or entity with more power.

The dynamics at work began to wear on Travis. He started to lose sleep. He felt irked. In fact, Travis woke up in the middle of the night thinking about his relationship with Alan. He wondered if he was built for office politics. He wasn't sure this was a game he was willing to play.

Travis came to coaching soon after. Despite Alan's lack of self-awareness as an executive, his firm made coaching available for those who were interested in it. After realizing that he was having trouble navigating his relationship with Alan, Travis asked for some support.

"How do you like your job?" I asked Travis when we first met.

Travis paused for a moment, then swallowed hard. He looked sad, even a little teary.

"This was exactly the job I wanted most out of business school," he said. "A lot of my friends were envious that I got this job so quickly, and I felt like I had really made it by landing this role. I imagined myself here staying for a while, maybe rising up the ranks. Now, though, I'm not so sure. I'm not enjoying myself very much, and I wonder if this is really the place for me after all."

What's going on here: the psychological and relational dimension

As I considered Travis's situation, it felt important to acknowledge that there were different things going on simultaneously. There was a psychological dimension to what he was experiencing as well as something relational, which is generally true of organizational life.

Using the language of Gestalt, the two psychological interruptions that seemed most apparent for Travis were the dynamics of confluence and deflection. Similar to those profiled in previous chapters, Travis felt a pressure to go along to get along in a confluent way in order to be successful at his firm. He had a sense—perhaps accurately—that if he suspended his own needs and made himself confluent with Alan, then all would be OK.

Travis also had a related habit of deflecting. The act of deflection is our unconscious attempt to take the heat out of a situation. We avoid what feels uncomfortable for us. Think of the person who smiles when they are telling you something that is difficult for them to say, or the person who tells a joke when things get a little tense in the room, or the person that tells you how they are doing but not really. Deflection keeps us safe (or so we think), but it also means we avoid the thing that is most true for us to say.

I realized that Travis was caught in a common, and even somewhat predictable, moment in organizational life. He was faced with the question of whether he could actually be himself and speak truthfully—especially to someone in power—or whether he would have to go along to get along. By being confluent and deflecting his own needs, Travis was trying to avoid conflict with Alan. He also concluded that this was what he'd have to do to "get ahead."

To be sure, human relationships are frequently reciprocal in nature, especially in organizational life. Balancing what we give and what we get is as relevant at work as it is in marriage and friendships. We must compromise in relationships. We must consider what we're willing to give in order to get what we want. While we can hope that our relationships are not solely transactional, we must acknowledge that sometimes we have to give something now to get something in the future. The transactional dimension to work relationships can be even more intense, especially when it relates to those who have more positional power than we do.

For Travis to navigate these choices, he first had to discern which battles were worth fighting and which weren't. He also had to decide to what extent he was going to play politics and continue to be confluent or deflect. Knowing when and how to strike a conscious balance between the two would be key.

Bringing awareness to our habits

As the coaching with Travis began, I introduced the concepts of confluence and deflection. Travis could recognize himself in these habits, and I wanted to bring his attention to just how often he was acting in a confluent way or was deflecting and didn't even know it.

These coping mechanisms are not always unhealthy or unhelpful; we are looking for when we behave in chronic and unconscious ways. When we do so, our coping mechanisms (also called defenses) are controlling us more than we are controlling them.

Travis was raised in a family where there was very little overt conflict. He also felt a subtle pressure to go along to get along, and that suited his easygoing personality well. He was not in the habit of being vocal about a difference of opinion, and mostly it served him in his relationships. While the confluence exhibited by my other clients profiled in this book was born more out of fear and unsafe family dynamics, this was not Travis's reality. Nonetheless, he had a habit of acting in a confluent way to be liked and to keep things calm around him.

Travis and I talked about the pressure to go along and to be confluent at work, especially with those in power. He was not alone in having this experience, and sadly, it's my observation that too many people in power are deluded enough to believe that everyone has to agree with them to be good "team players."

I don't see it this way. In my experience, good leaders have to have stable enough egos to be able to tolerate when people disagree with them and to invite different perspectives that intellectually challenge and "stress test" their ideas. When employees do disagree, they need to do it respectfully, so that it doesn't feel like a fight for control.

Disagreeing with his boss was especially difficult for Travis, who was younger and didn't particularly want to play political chess or be perceived as The Angry Black Man either. He wanted to enjoy his work and do it well. He needed support in navigating the sensitive terrain of his current workplace.

"Travis, I'd love to explore a little bit about how you're seeing yourself and the workplace," I said. "Is fair to say that you've gotten along well with people at work?"

"Oh yeah, definitely, I'm not really interested in confrontation," he said. "Generally, relationships come easily. My parents always taught me to respect people in positions of authority, and I've always had really good relationships with teachers, professors, colleagues."

"And with Alan?"

Travis leaned forward, clasped his hands, and put his elbows on his knees.

"With Alan, I didn't feel respected, so it made me feel some hurt and frustration, even some anger," he said, in a serious, level tone. "More than anything, my parents taught me not to make waves, to go along, and over time, I'd be rewarded. I've taken that really seriously. My dad worked at a city agency all his life, and that mostly worked for him. I thought it would work for me, too."

"But it sounds like that may not be your way?"

"No, I suppose not."

"Is it fair to say that you're trying to walk the line between being accepted as a Black man in a largely white office with the need to enjoy yourself in this workplace and succeed on your own terms without playing games?"

"Yes, yes, exactly!" he said, leaning back and looking relieved.

"And what I'm also hearing from you is it's hard to know whether this is about being a person of color," I said. "It feels more like this is about Alan's lack of emotional maturity, huh?"

"Yes."

During our sessions, I asked Travis to become aware of when and how he deflected. I asked him to notice how often he smiled, as he spoke, when things weren't actually funny. How he softened his words frequently—the result being that the watered-down version of reality that he communicated was hard to follow. I also brought his attention to how he would deflect talking about his actual experience in the moment.

Often clients don't want to discuss what they're actually feeling in a given moment, but they want to tell you the stories of their lives. This is deeply ingrained and is so basic to the way we communicate that it can seem like no big deal. But over time and done chronically, deflection like this can amount to a big deal.

It means that instead of experiencing ourselves in the present moment, we live in the past or the future—neither of which is actually as "real" as we think. It means that we are a little out of step with what is most alive—the present moment, and in our communications, we end up avoiding conflict and watering down what is most true.

With Travis, for instance, his common rejoinder was "it's all good," and it turned out that he was a chronic deflector. Often seen as the funny one in a group, he had a talent for making serious things entertaining. This served a purpose, as people found him likable, easy to be around, and fun. But Travis often bit his tongue about what he really thought and felt, and while this mostly served him socially, in the office, it was becoming a liability—and it was literally keeping him up at night.

He was not sure that deflecting was serving him anymore, especially with Alan, and he did not know if he wanted to make the trade-off necessary to appease him. He was warming up to the idea of not turning down the heat quite so much.

With time, Travis grew to realize how often he was accustomed to deflecting—how often he avoided difficult conversations by using humor and how often he smiled when things weren't actually pleasing or funny to him. He also learned, through our sessions, that speaking truthfully felt good, even if at first it felt uncomfortable and new. He practiced saying things aloud in our sessions that he wanted to say to Alan—for example, "I respect your experience on this, Alan, but I don't agree with your recommendation."

Travis and I also discussed the trade-offs that he faced at work. He could continue with his habits of confluence and deflection, and he might keep losing sleep and feeling frustrated. He could speak truth to power out of frustration (specifically, Alan), and he could potentially risk his reputation or his job. We explored the in-between space, too—one that I believe many mature professionals must learn to inhabit: speaking truthfully, as often as possible, from a conscious and caring place so that one's integrity is respected.

Travis agreed, but he also wanted to go along to get along at times to support an ongoing working relationship—and to get his own needs met at a future point. The reality is, sometimes forms of confluence and deflection may be necessary if we are to be successful in organizational life.

Navigating organizational hierarchy

With the support of coaching, Travis practiced what it was like to speak with candor, truth, and care. And as the months progressed, I heard how Travis was starting to show up at work.

He wasn't muting his thoughts but articulating them. He realized that disagreeing with Alan publicly was more loaded than disagreeing with him privately, a strategy we might call "positive politics." Travis had more opportunities to practice with George, who was more easygoing than Alan, which allowed Travis to take chances and be more honest in group settings.

"Would you say you're experimenting with ways of communicating that are more contextual, depending on whom you're dealing with?" I asked.

"Exactly," Travis replied. "I used to think politics was all B.S. and that I didn't want to have to change my message in any way because then I wouldn't be me. I'm realizing I can still be me and speak truthfully, but I'm also learning to choose my moments."

Speaking truthfully didn't mean he had to share every thought in his head, in every moment. It meant being in touch with himself and also able to tolerate uncomfortable feelings like fear and anxiety that might arise.

Behaving differently to get something different

Travis was a good student of himself and of organizational life. By bringing awareness to his habits of confluence and deflection, he practiced discernment. He could consciously choose to go along or to refrain from speaking his truth and know that he was making that choice out of a desire to build and maintain important work relationships.

As we've seen in another chapter, I believe that the best, and most mature, communication, is done with truth *and* care. If we avoid the truth again and again, we betray ourselves, and we may even have trouble knowing what is true for us over time. And if we avoid communicating with care for the other person and for our relationship, then what we share may come out with a harshness that we don't intend or that can hurt others.

Travis also learned how habitually he deflected and avoided difficult feelings and conversations. He realized that while deeply familiar, deflection was having a negative effect on his life—not just professionally, but personally. He had assumed the role of entertainer in friend groups and at work without tracking its cost.

After becoming more aware of his chronic smile and laugh in social and work situations, Travis started to do these things less often. He started to smile and laugh less automatically in social settings to hide other emotions. He allowed himself to experience boredom, confusion, embarrassment, frustration, and sadness, which didn't always need to be shared with others but created a more honest relationship with himself.

Travis said being more emotionally honest and vulnerable was good for his relationship with his girlfriend, too.

"I've always had a little bit of a shield up. Through this process, though, I'm starting to realize that's not so good for me, and I need to show up more honestly with my girlfriend, too," he told me. "That means sometimes telling her if she hurts my feelings, which I would never have done before. I'm talking to her more, and she says she feels closer to me. This actually can bring me closer to the people I love."

Speaking truthfully with care to Alan was not entirely easy for Travis. Alan did not react well to being challenged, but Travis was bold enough to schedule a time to speak with Alan. He wanted to share with Alan what he had learned in coaching and asked if Alan would be willing to be more open to Travis's difference of opinion.

On reflection, Alan could see Travis's point. He even revealed to Travis that in his own executive coaching process he was focusing on reducing his anger management and defensiveness at work. "I was really impressed and realized that everybody has to make adjustments," Travis said. "I didn't think this guy would ever say something like that publicly, and it makes me feel more hopeful about my future there."

Travis wasn't sure how long he would stay at the firm, but he also wanted to be pragmatic along the way. With more care than ever, Travis selected when he wanted to take someone on—usually Alan—and when he could let go.

Travis ended up staying with the firm for a few more years and was even promoted along the way. When he decided to leave, it was not out of fear, and it was not out of avoidance. An exciting offer had come along, and Travis wanted to take on the challenge now that he was equipped with leadership skills that allowed him to consciously make hard decisions that felt true to himself.

He was glad he had stayed to practice speaking honestly to Alan and others because along the way Travis became more than the easygoing guy who went along to get along. He was now perceived as having maturity, integrity, and clarity. In other words, he'd grown up at work before their eyes.

► REFLECTIONS ◄

- Do I avoid speaking my truth in work meetings? How often do I bite my tongue? Why?

- Did I come from a family where difficult topics were avoided or where it was threatening to speak truthfully?

- Am I a chronic smiler or someone who makes jokes to "lighten the mood"?

- Do I tell myself I have to be political to be successful in my job?

- Am I OK with the trade-offs involved in being political?

- What do I imagine would happen if I spoke more truthfully, especially to those in power? Am I curious about how that might feel?

► PRACTICES ◄

- Practice speaking truth with care. This means that you don't have to share every thought in your head, and you don't need to cushion the blow so much that people don't actually understand what you are saying. Speaking truthfully means we discern what's important for us to say and what we would regret not saying.

- Practice showing up in your work interactions from a place of trust versus fear. Ask yourself: *What would I say right now if I weren't scared? How could I say that thing clearly and with care for others?* Practice communicating from a place of pleasing yourself versus pleasing others. It can be helpful to rehearse difficult conversations in advance.

- Practice tolerating difficult feelings that emerge when you're tempted to deflect or be confluent. It's not that these feelings are bad; it's just that you're not used to feeling them. Consider that they're just feelings—like fear, confusion, anxiety—and that you can feel them and breathe instead of avoiding them.

- Practice speaking truthfully in your organization and see what happens over time. If you are implicitly or explicitly penalized, consider the following: Could your delivery be more respectful so that people could actually hear you without getting defensive? Might there be a bit of an edge to your voice that you could mitigate?

- If you feel you've been respectful, and you get that feedback from others, then also consider whether you want to stay working in a place where you are punished for speaking honestly? Consider whether there might be a place for you where you don't have to do such a twisting of yourself to get along.

- If you think you need to build the skill of having difficult conversations, find a helpful resource like *Nonviolent Communication* by Marshall Rosenberg. There are many great books, podcasts, and workshops available to help you learn and practice this skill.

► **EXPERIMENTS** ◄

- Begin by bringing your awareness to how frequently you hold back saying what's true for you. Ask why you do that and notice how it physically feels in your body to hold back. Notice any tension, energy, sensations, or feelings that are present for you.

- Start small: You don't have to say the most inconvenient truth on day one or the thing that's going to be most difficult for people to hear. But why not try by speaking honestly about something with smaller stakes? See what that's like.

- Notice if there are "sacred cows" in your organization—things that no one questions but might be worth questioning. Consider asking why things are done in a certain way, how decisions are made, and so on.

Chapter 7

People Think I'm a Jerk

ED WAS KIND OF A jerk. Everyone he worked with said so. A vice president of marketing at a media company and in his mid-forties, Ed didn't actually care that everyone thought he was a jerk, and needless to say, the few coaching sessions I spent with Ed were not easy or enjoyable. Far from it.

One of the first things I ask anyone who is interested in executive coaching or is required to attend by their boss is: "Are you interested in learning about yourself?"

"Do you want to change and grow?" I ask. "You don't have to have all of the answers, but if you're not interested, this is probably not going to work."

Ed wanted coaching because his boss told him that it was a necessary step before securing his next promotion. Ed wanted me to teach him a better "script" to use with his team, but he had no interest in developing real care or empathy for his colleagues.

"They're mostly idiots," he said.

Coaching with Ed didn't last long. I am not an acting teaching or a script writer, and I'm not all that interested in helping people fake sincerity or care for others.

Mark, on the other hand, was different.

In his early forties and of German-American descent, Mark worked at a software company as a director of Research and Development. His reputation preceded him as conscientious, cerebral, and a hard nut to crack. He had a cool demeanor but, in contrast to Ed, he also had a shy, mild-mannered sincerity. He was receiving coaching because his boss, Emily, had had such a positive experience of executive coaching as a tool for self-acceptance that she asked her direct reports to go through the process as well. She felt that it would make them all better people, and therefore, better leaders.

"Coaching hasn't worked so well for me in the past, but I'm open to giving it another try," he said. "I'm afraid I don't know that much about being a good manager, and I want to get better."

Genuinely interested in improving his interpersonal skills at work, Mark was curious about finding ways to grow. That's all we needed to get started.

Egotism

Coaching for leaders is frequently preceded by a thorough 360 review, a systematic process whereby we collect anonymous feedback about the leader from their peers, direct reports, and those who manage them.

Mark's 360 was pretty bad. He had some of the lowest scores I had seen in a while. While his bosses loved him, Mark's peers were deeply frustrated by him. He scored very poorly in areas like authenticity, self-awareness, and relating to others. He was described as arrogant, critical, and autocratic.

The comments bore this out: "He thinks he's the smartest guy in the room." "Mark always has to get his way, no matter what." "He bulldozes his way through meetings. There's no point in trying to stop him." "He rolls his eyes when he thinks no one's looking, but we see him."

In Gestalt terms, the emotional challenge at play here is "egotism," an orientation toward the world that assumes that our needs and experiences are central, to the exclusion of others.

Most of us guide our lives with reference to our values, our impulses, and our needs, but as we grow, we realize that we share space with others and that their needs and their feelings count. Those who suffer from egotism haven't quite made that shift. They still negotiate the world without much reference to the perspective of others.

Because Mark's 360 data was so critical, I didn't feel it was right to introduce it in the first session. Instead, I took some time to get to know him. One of the things our initial session confirmed was that Mark was smart. He had been through four years of medical school and only quit because he couldn't stand the sight of blood. After becoming a teacher, he subsequently moved into software development, where his analytical skills helped revolutionize the department in which he worked. It was easy to see why his bosses might speak favorably about him.

But alongside all of this success, Mark left a trail of hurt and frustrated coworkers. If he heard an idea he disagreed with in a meeting, he would roll his eyes or frown or even laugh. Because he was a fast thinker, he would talk a solution through quickly and would get impatient with anyone who couldn't keep up. He hoarded the most complex work for himself, leaving his direct reports with the impression that he didn't think them capable of it. He was seen as distant and cold and prepared to stomp over anyone to get his way.

How others see us

When it came time to look at the report, I asked Mark if he had any guesses about what he was going to find. He had been coached before, so he had some sense that he was capable of rubbing people the wrong way. Moreover, he talked about a vague feeling of unease that would frequently settle on him before he went to sleep each night. Though he couldn't quite put a finger on why, he knew that the day had not gone particularly well.

In my experience, the body doesn't lie. We don't always know what it's saying, but it regularly gives us information.

"Did you have a sense that things weren't going so well?" I asked Mark.

"You know, it's funny because it's been several months, but I leave work and I kind of feel one way. Then, on the subway ride home, I start getting a sinking feeling that I may have messed up," he said.

It was like a little voice in his head was suggesting something was off. I had a clinical supervisor who talked about "the intelligence of feelings." Many of us are apt to dismiss that vague sense of guilt or unhappiness, when the truth is that it often carries valuable data.

The thing about these 360 reviews is that they are extremely robust. Respondents are asked a series of qualitative and quantitative questions, and the collated results are benchmarked against a database of more than 300,000 leaders worldwide.

If you end up in the lowest percentile, if you end up among those held in the lowest regard by their peers, you can't simply dismiss it and say, "Oh, they just don't like me." You have to sit up and take notice. And if, like Mark, data is your thing, it is even more difficult to reject the results as subjective or unscientific.

I'm always a little nervous when I'm handing out a report that's this bad, and this was no exception. First, I shared a generic 360 report so Mark and I could discuss the format and what we were going to be looking at.

Next, I handed Mark's report to him a little slowly. He sat diagonally across the office table from me. I didn't know how he would react. Would he get defensive? Sad? Anyone could see at first glance that the negative feedback was significant and positive feedback was mostly missing.

Mark examined it intently, without betraying his emotions. As he read, he looked like a teenager leaning back in his chair and tipping its front two legs precariously up in the air.

"This doesn't look so good, does it?" he said. It sounded like a statement more than a question.

Reading his review was a sobering moment for Mark. It was a wake-up call. Here was incontrovertible evidence that he was failing as a leader.

The job has changed

One of the great things about the Gestalt technique (and much of psychotherapy) is that everything can be "grist for the mill." What's happening in the room is live information; it's relevant data. And in Gestalt specifically, we use ourselves as an "instrument": We take note of our observations and pay attention to how we are affected by the other.

As I got to know Mark, I started paying close attention to his body language. I listened to him as the *storyteller* as much as I listened to his *story*. Mark had a mischievous glint in his eye. He'd laugh when things weren't funny; he'd roll his eyes a little.

One day, as we discussed his perceptions of one of his peers, he gave a little laugh, so I stopped him mid-flow.

"What just happened? What are you doing right now?" I asked.

"Excuse me?" he replied.

"You were talking about Emma, about something she said, and you laughed," I said. "Why? Do you think she's wrong?"

Mark was taken aback and sat staring at me for a moment like a deer in headlights.

"Well, yes," he said eventually. "I do think she's wrong."

I looked back at him.

It was a little bit of a gotcha moment.

"Oh," he said. "I see."

This was also an example of us making the unconscious conscious. Indeed, Mark was not aware that his criticism of Emma was so apparent. He thought he was keeping it to himself, like a thought bubble no one could see, but he had something like a tell in poker. His tell, or giveaway, was that he would kind of smile or laugh at slightly inappropriate moments. By sharing my observation with him, I wanted to increase his self-awareness, and I also wanted to suggest that I might not be the only one around him picking up on the small signals he was sending.

Mark got a little sheepish as it dawned on him that his criticism of Emma bordered on disdain, especially his delivery, and it's what people like her were picking up on at work.

Building empathy: What is it like for others to work with me?

If egotism is the challenge, one of the primary antidotes is to build real empathy for others. Mark and I began to explore this question: What might it *feel like* to work with him?

I asked him to imagine he was one of his colleagues: "Let's say you're in a meeting and Mark walks in. How does he affect you?"

This approach can be helpful if the client is willing to be imaginative, willing to experiment.

I added, "OK, Mark just rolled his eyes after I said something. Is it because of what I said? Does he think I'm stupid? Or Mark just interrupted me, he cut me off. Does he not respect my opinion?"

Mark looked thoughtful after he considered these possibilities more carefully.

"You know, I'm not very sensitive myself, so if someone rolled their eyes at me in a meeting, I wouldn't actually care all that much," he said. "But I guess a lot of other people aren't built that way, and I imagine I'm hurting their feelings."

He paused and looked thoughtful.

"Maybe I am a big jerk," he said. "I might not want to offer my ideas to someone like me, either."

Looking at those frowns, laughs, snide comments, and interruptions from the point of view of those on the receiving end helped open Mark's eyes to his impact on his colleagues.

There is a popular leadership book by Marshall Goldsmith, a renowned executive coach, with a beautifully simple and instructive title: *What Got You Here Won't Get You There*. I don't often have to do much explaining of this concept for leaders to get it. Many leaders, like Mark, have succeeded at work because of their intellect and technical skills. They've been promoted because they produced excellent results.

What this old-school model doesn't take into account, though, is that it is one's relationship skills that create our success, increasingly and especially at the higher levels of an organization. It is less and less about one's technical skills, but more about whether a leader can build trust and inspire others. The most effective and inspiring leaders don't coerce others. They use healthy forms of social influence that stem from competence and trust.

Mark's success had relied on his technical skills, but succeeding as a leader wasn't going to be about technical skills; it would be about forming trusting relationships with fellow staff. This was what it took for him to *get there*—the next stop on his journey as a leader and as a person.

For our next session, I gave him some homework.

"Gather data, then make inferences about what motivates each of your colleagues," I said. "Try to understand how they are experiencing the world. What's going on with them today? How did they wake up? What's important in their world? What's stressing them out?"

Mark was intrigued. He was analytical, after all. Data spoke to him, and because he was a good student, it could help accelerate things. On the other hand, and like the kid in the back of the class, I knew he would not be motivated unless he bought into something. We were building rapport and mutual respect, but I sensed he was still skeptical.

"Do I tell people I'm doing this experiment?" he asked me.

"That's up to you," I said. "But just observe, listen, and try to make inferences."

Honoring the I-Thou relationship

The philosopher Martin Buber talked about the sanctity of the "I-Thou" relationship. As human beings moving through the world, we tend to be very focused on ourselves as the "I," and everyone else is in danger of being reduced to an "it," a means to an end or an obstacle. Others cease to be complex, three-dimensional beings and become defined only in terms of *our* needs. Buber's suggestion is that we move into something much more existentially rich when we recognize that every relationship is an "I-Thou."

As Mark started his homework of observing his colleagues and imagining their motivations and need, he began to be affected by them. They had ideas of their own. They had desires of their own, wishes of their own, and feelings of their own. In his mind, he began to see that they weren't just obstacles if they didn't agree with him or think as quickly as he did.

Mark's growth was further supported by his experience as a devoted, sincere father and husband who was invested in the happiness of his family. Mark was somber and reflective as he told me about how he had recently experienced a difficult period while one of his children had been seriously ill.

"My son developed very weird symptoms, and we were at the doctor on and off for a couple of months," he said. "For a while, it was unclear what was going on, and I was very scared."

In fact, whenever we spoke about his family, Mark became animated and tender, and it became increasingly clear to me that he *did know* how to be empathic and caring toward others. He practiced it daily at home. He just needed to practice some of this same care and consideration with his colleagues at work. He started to learn that they needed his appreciation as much as his family did.

It's also important to note that Mark, for all his flaws, was an excellent student. He was genuinely open to change. He shared his coaching goals with the people around him at work, and he asked them regularly for feedback. He started to open meetings by collecting ideas from others, and instead of explaining what would happen, he created more opportunities for idea exchange and discussion.

Critically, he began to see the risk attached to continuing to behave as he had been. He did not want to lose smart, talented people. He didn't want them to decide, *that's it, I've had enough. I'm out of here.*

When Mark opened up to the truth, which was that people left his company feeling sad, hurt, and demoralized, he *cared*. He wanted it to stop.

He cared about the impact he was having on people. The problem was that he had been only dimly aware of it. Becoming conscious of that impact suddenly opened up a world of options for him, options that did not exist when he was blind to the impact of his actions.

"I know I haven't been the best manager, but I hate the idea that people would be quitting because of me, and I'm making this a bad place to work," he said.

"I'm hearing that you care about the effect you're having on people, and you don't want them to leave. Is that right?" I asked.

"Yes," he replied, matter-of-factly. He could joke around a lot, but it was clear that he took this seriously.

Looking out for unintended consequences

One day, as our work continued, we returned to one of the themes from his 360 review—why he sometimes hoarded work for himself.

"What do you think is going on for you when you hoard work?" I asked. "What do you think that's about?"

"It's probably a few things," he said. "I really like the quants part of my job, so it's fun sometimes to delve into a problem until it's solved. Also, when I'm really running up against hard deadlines, I don't want to burden somebody with last-minute work. I know I can take it home, and truthfully, sometimes I hoard work because I know I'm going to do it right. I don't want to go through the double work of correcting other people's mistakes."

I nodded in encouragement.

"OK. It sounds like you have some interesting reasons, and your intention is being efficient and not burdening other people. But what might be the unintended consequences of doing this?" I asked.

He looked away and thought for a minute.

"They might think I'm kind of a ball hog and want all the interesting work for myself," he said, then took another minute to think. "They might also think that I think I'm the smartest guy in the room, and maybe that I think they're not very smart?"

"Interesting," I said. "And how does that affect you to imagine others thinking you're judging them for not being smart enough?"

"Well, that doesn't feel good. It certainly doesn't feel like the kind of manager I want to be," he replied.

"It's probably fair to say that training them to solve problems as well as you do might take some extra time and might not always be efficient. But is that something you're willing to do as their manager?" I asked. "It's part of your job. Are you interested in that part?"

"I used to be a teacher, and that was what I liked the most. So yeah, I'm willing to do that."

Mark had begun to see that by hoarding work for himself, he was withholding opportunities for growth from his team. In effect, he was telling his team that he didn't believe they were competent, and that he didn't want to develop them.

Here was another of Mark's *aha* moments, and one that was easy to act on. He immediately began delegating more work.

Building empathy and psychological safety

In 2015 Google published the results of a mammoth, two-year study on team performance called "Project Aristotle." They found that the best teams demonstrate a high level of psychological safety; in fact, it was the most relevant predictor of team performance.

What does that mean? In successful teams, the members are socially attuned to each other. They have a sensitivity to each other's needs. In psychologically unsafe teams, one or two people can dominate, leaving the rest feeling intimidated and unable to contribute. On psychologically safe teams, there's no embarrassment or shame in asking a question, in being yourself, in voicing an idea that turns out to be bad, or in making a mistake and learning from it.

For someone like Mark, knowing that these ideas were underpinned by evidence-based research was key to his buy-in. Remember, this was someone with a special relationship with data. He needed to know the science before he could feel motivated to act.

Leaders—not just Mark—frequently discount the impact they can have on a room with their tone, body language, words, or pacing. But leaders set the tone. If the boss comes into a meeting agitated or prickly, it puts everyone else on edge. This can seriously diminish the level of psychological safety in a room before a word is spoken.

As leaders shift toward a more relational way of leading, and only if they practice with sincerity and consistency, they can earn the respect of their peers and staff. With time, teams start to believe their leaders actually care about them, their careers, and their growth. Staff want to contribute and stay in organizations where their managers care.

It's an old but true adage: "People don't leave organizations, they leave managers." By taking responsibility for the effect they have on others, leaders are able to create the conditions for psychological safety and healthy collaboration.

These little habits—rolling your eyes, laughing inappropriately—are deeply ingrained. Stopping these habits is not easy, but it begins with self-awareness, which is the foundation for emotional intelligence and for effective leadership. As a result of difficult feedback, leaders often must realize that their existing drivers—efficiency, getting things done, self-reliance—need to be reset, and some of their well-worn habits need to change.

I gave Mark another homework assignment.

"Over the next two weeks, pay attention to the level of psychological safety in the room," I said. "Fine-tune your radar. Observe how people act, observe how *you* act. If you're so inclined, experiment in little ways to do things differently."

Mark's department had a lot of meetings, and he came back to me with examples from half a dozen. His findings: He tended to always speak first, which affected the entire room and often discouraged others from expressing competing ideas. He experimented with waiting to speak, sometimes going last in the group.

He had usually disagreed with others by saying "no, but," and basically debating them instead of building on their ideas. He tried replacing this simple phrase with "yes, and."

"Wow, this stuff doesn't have to be so complicated," he said. "How could this not have dawned on me earlier?"

"It's actually less work sometimes to be a good leader if you take seriously that what you're trying to do is to hear from other people," I said. "You don't have to prove that you're the smartest person anymore. You can sit back, listen, and consider what others have to say. "

In other words, he didn't have to run around with the ball. He could pass it around and spend more time on the sidelines.

We worked on helping Mark break through those moments and develop new reflexes that created psychological safety for the people around him. Instead of rolling his eyes when he felt impatient, he would breathe and nod. Instead of furrowing his brow when he disagreed with someone, he would breathe and sit back in his chair. When he listened to people, he learned to nod more and not cross his arms. He could still use his sense of humor, but in a more mature way that didn't make other people feel bad.

We all know how hard it is to break a habit. A smoker setting out to quit will replace the habit rather than go cold turkey. *I'm going to exercise every time I feel the need for a cigarette. I'm going to meditate rather than light up.* It is very difficult to stop a habit, but you can replace it with a healthier one. That's exactly what Mark was trying to do.

Journaling as a key support for growth

I recommend journaling to pretty much all of the leaders whom I coach. Journaling allows you to keep track of your intentions and your progress, and by providing you with a reliable record of your lived experience, it accelerates your introspection and facilitates empathy building.

Unfortunately, only some of my clients actually take up my invitation. But Mark? Mark was someone who took his homework seriously. He was so keen to grow up, to become a better leader, that he embraced anything that might help.

Each day, on the subway home from Manhattan to Queens, he diligently posted the details of his day into his phone. These entries, which he sent to me, were invariably self-critical: *I didn't do well at that meeting. I spoke too much. I could see where Jim was going with his point and I just shouted him down.* He started tracking the energy with which he approached his meetings, his beliefs and goals, as well as how others seemed to be reacting to him. He also started noting where his own changes were starting to take effect.

"I'm seeing that I can really change the dynamics of a meeting by doing a few small things, and people seem to be reacting positively," he told me.

"That's great," I said, smiling.

"In fact, a few people have come up to me after meetings and remarked how well they went. One person pulled me over privately to say that whatever was going on in coaching seemed to be paying off. And this was someone I used to butt heads with all the time in staff meetings."

While the "I-Thou" relationship covered the attitude piece, the other behavioral dimension that I wanted Mark to address related to the distinction between advocacy mode and inquiry mode, something discussed by author and team expert Patrick Lencioni in his work with teams. In most human interactions, we are usually in one of these modes of being. In advocacy mode, we are focused on advancing our own views, winning the argument. In inquiry mode, it's the opposite. We're trying to understand and integrate another person's contribution. We're trying to be influenced by others.

Mark was a natural advocate; he could convince anybody of anything. By noticing this behavioral inclination, and being aware of its opposite, Mark had a new perspective on his actions. He could pull back and say to himself, *Oh, I'm in advocacy mode at the moment, not inquiry*. Daily journaling gave these observations greater durability and force, and allowed him to get to know himself a little better.

This is how empathy is built. It is built by noticing, as well as we can, how others are acting and feeling around us. It's about making adjustments in the spirit of better, healthier relationships.

A fresh 360

When we ran Mark's 360 assessment a second time, nine months later, the results were markedly different. And the comments told a story all of their own: "I can see how hard Mark is trying." "He listens to me now; I mean he genuinely listens." "Mark is a much easier guy to be around. I can see that he's really working to be a better person and manager."

In addition to Mark, we coached five other people on the leadership team of which he was a member. During that process, we often got unsolicited comments, all along the same lines: "Mark's coaching is really making a difference with him." "This guy is really trying." "He's not bulldozing conversations, he's listening more in meetings, he's asking more questions." "He admits when he screws up and apologizes if he needs to."

And that vague sense of unease that accompanied him to bed each night? It disappeared.

It would be wrong to think that everyone lived happily ever after here. As is true in the world of addiction, relapse is part of the recovery process.

Mark says that if he had the budget, he would remain in coaching for the rest of his life—just as someone with an injured leg may need ongoing physical therapy to enable them to walk well. I recommend continuing journaling as way to help embed positive behaviors and attitudes. I also think it's important to have a trusted peer or someone in your work environment who can give you honest feedback—someone who will answer honestly when you ask how you came off in that meeting.

Understanding that growth is not linear has been helpful for Mark, particularly after meetings or interactions in which his old behaviors reasserted themselves, often under stress. Recovery is not effortless, nor is it ever complete. An alcoholic won't say he's recovered, he'll say he's in recovery—his sobriety is a daily practice. So it is with Mark, who tries hard to stay intentional and empathic now, one day at a time.

► REFLECTIONS ◄

At the end of any interaction at work (or in life), consider the following questions:

- What did I notice about my tone, my words, and my nonverbal communication during that meeting?

- How did others seem to respond to me?

- Did I add to the sense of psychological safety in this situation or did I detract from it?

- How do I feel about myself after the interaction? How do I imagine others feel?

- Did I fall back on old habits or did I try something new?

- If I messed up, how might I rectify that?

- What do I want and why? And am I acting in a way that will get me closer to what I want?

► PRACTICES ◄

- Daily journaling is an excellent means of accelerating self-awareness and helping you to change what needs to be changed.

- Read articles and books that can help you to step outside of yourself. Mark found that *Leadership and Self-Deception*, authored by the Arbinger Institute, helped him to realize that he often saw people as a means to an end and that he was "in the box." It is only when you recognize that you're "in the box" that you have the freedom to step outside of it. Other helpful resources include *The Fearless Organization* by Amy Edmondson and information about "Project Aristotle" on the Google website.

▶   **EXPERIMENTS**   ◀

Through his behavior, Mark was unwittingly sending a signal to his team that he didn't care. If you find yourself in this situation, do something different:

- Approach interactions with positive intentions. Plan for being intentional, kind, and collaborative.

- Listen more than you speak.

- Realize that in conversation we tend to be either in inquiry mode or advocacy mode. Inquiry mode tends to bring people closer to us. We ask for more information, and we try to learn what others think and why they think it. Bring your attention to the mode you're in. If you're often in advocacy mode (focused on your own views), experiment with inquiry mode (and vice versa).

- Rotate who owns and facilitates meetings among your staff.

- Shift your thinking from the belief that you must do everything yourself.

- Practice sharing power—for how meetings are run, how decisions are made, and so on.

- Remind yourself regularly that you don't have all the answers, even if you are very smart.

Chapter 8

People Don't Trust Me

AS AN ACCOUNT DIRECTOR AT a prestigious Manhattan advertising agency, Dennis's job was to make sure his clients were happy. He worked hard to ensure they felt understood and that his team produced fresh advertising campaigns designed to position his clients well.

Dennis provided a level of service that his clients highly valued; he'd get on calls with them at all hours of the day and night, often to assuage their concerns or anxieties. Excellent client management was important to Dennis. His high-profile accounts represented millions of dollars of revenue.

An attractive, slender man of Chinese-American descent in his forties, Dennis regularly wore tailor-made suits punctuated with stylish cufflinks. His Italian dress shoes were always freshly polished. He used business jargon fluidly and sincerely—words like "synergy" and "top line growth" came naturally and often when he spoke.

When I met Dennis, he had been offered executive coaching as part of a senior leadership team initiative to create more employee engagement within the firm. He had never had coaching before, and he was not sure what to expect. I began by speaking to his colleagues confidentially about their perceptions of Dennis so I could get a sense of how to best help Dennis grow. When I presented my results to Dennis, he was shocked.

"Wow, it's really hard to hear this. I've gotten so many stellar reviews from my managers, and I think my clients are really pleased with my work," he said. "I had no idea people weren't happy working for me."

A lack of trust

It was clear that Dennis's clients loved him, and nothing in my interviews challenged that idea. Dennis was seen as an excellent salesperson, able to reassure and influence his clients, while selling enormous, ongoing projects that kept teams of people at the firm busy with billable time.

But the people who reported to Dennis at the agency did have a problem with him: They didn't quite trust him.

They couldn't always put their finger on it, but throughout the interviews, his colleagues told me they felt they didn't really know who Dennis *was*. They wondered if he was maybe a bit two-faced. He was charming with clients and for senior management, but they didn't feel they knew what he stood for; they didn't feel "seen" by him.

His direct reports worried about whether he was genuinely looking after their interests and speaking up for them with management. They also wondered if he cared about their career growth and supporting their success, or if he was just trying to make himself look good.

When we instinctively sense that we are not seeing the "real person," it makes us wonder what they are up to. Are they playing a game with us? Are they polite and charming to our face but undermining us at every opportunity behind our backs? Are they using us in some way? All of this, naturally, is work, too, and takes mental energy away from our actual work.

Most of Dennis's staff were Millennials at least ten years younger than him. They told me consistently that while he was someone they could turn to for technical guidance, he was not someone they viewed as a trusted mentor who took an interest in their lives or careers. You don't get to be in Dennis's position at a high-profile agency without being tough and competitive. They didn't have a problem with that; they respected it.

He was good with the business, and there was nothing abrasive about his management style, but he had put up walls to keep others out. It seemed no one would dream of approaching Dennis with a more personal issue. They didn't feel drawn to him in that way, and they didn't think he'd be interested in having anything but a client-related conversation with them.

Dennis just seemed to them to be . . . a bit hollow.

A false self

As Dennis and I began our coaching work together, it was clear that he was truly surprised and confused by the results of my interviews. He was highly accomplished. He had worked hard to be brilliant at his job and to do everything right, and he had succeeded.

His clients and management loved him, and he was positioned to be a senior executive in the firm. What was the problem? What else was he supposed to do?

Dennis was good at presenting the image that he knew would be appropriate to his role and the situation. He could go into any encounter, be brilliant and charismatic, and come away with the result he was seeking. In our coaching sessions, though, he looked uncomfortable. He didn't know what was expected or how he should behave.

The answer is, of course, that nothing is expected and there is no right way to behave when you're being coached. I just need people to be themselves and tell me about how they see their world.

Dennis didn't really have a mode for that. Our early conversations were plodding and went something like this:

"Tell me about yourself."

"I've been working at the firm for ten years now. I enjoy it. Things are going well."

"Tell me about well. What does that mean to you?"

"Well is fine. Everything is fine. I feel good."

We were making a lot of small talk and not a lot of progress. When conversation skims along the surface without any substance for too long, whether it's a conference cocktail party, neighborhood get-together, or a client session, I try to stay patient. But frankly, I get bored.

It became increasingly clear to me that Dennis had a strong "false self," which was described by psychoanalyst D.W. Winnicott as how some human beings habitually present a façade to others—usually in an effort to gain approval and avoid rejection. (Psychoanalytically speaking, we develop a false self when our true self wasn't adequately mirrored back to us or was rejected by our caregivers.)

Dennis acted in the way he thought would be valued and appreciated by his audience rather than in any genuine, spontaneous way. He was many things to many people—the perfect ambassador to his clients, the perfect executive to his bosses. But on a more personal level, his colleagues found it hard to say who Dennis was because, in a very real sense, he didn't present much more than a well-crafted image. He avoided any kind of genuine relational contact. He was never vulnerable.

In an old-school management paradigm, the quality of authenticity would have been seen as superfluous, unnecessary. That management model has changed. There been radical changes not only in what we do and how we do it, but also in the people we lead, are led by, and collaborate with.

New generations of workers look to their leaders to provide a supportive environment built on trust, and this is likely to be a permanent and fundamental shift in employee expectations. Embracing whole-person growth, where personal *and* professional growth are not separate but intertwined, is the way of the future. While that is true for every professional in the modern workplace, it's especially relevant for leaders like Dennis who serve or seek to serve as role models.

For new generations who expect authentic engagement, distant leaders cannot be supportive figures, especially if there is mistrust. Not only are they not seen as supportive, but they are seen as a potential threat. People expecting a degree of nurturing and support will not be able to thrive under this style of leadership. They are also highly likely to withhold or water down disagreement, feedback, or questions, and will eventually look for a better working environment elsewhere.

Starting the work together

Dennis and I met for two sessions per month. In the early stages, Dennis was very uneasy with the idea of opening up to me in any meaningful sense. It was clear that he was not used to "being seen" by others, and that included me.

As I asked, I also discovered that there was generally not much intimacy in Dennis's life. He was second-generation Chinese-American, the only son of immigrant parents. He still had contact with some college pals, but he did not have many close friends or a significant other. Dennis prided himself in being a bachelor, but he tended to talk about being single as if it were a role he played on a sitcom versus something he actually wanted.

He would say things like, "I went to a bar last night, and we ran into a celebrity who was really drunk. It was hilarious. We took a picture and posted it on Instagram."

Meanwhile, I'd sit there thinking, *what are we talking about right now and why?*

It also became increasingly clear that Dennis didn't know that much about himself. He did very little in the way of introspection. He saw his own life very much in terms of surface—he was "a successful advertising exec"—and he had little knowledge of or interest in what might lie behind that or be motivating his behavior at a deeper level.

A couple of sessions in, our exchanges were still feeling like a game of ping-pong, bouncing back and forth without any kind of victory in sight.

"Did you always want to be in advertising, Dennis?" I asked.

"Yes, I always knew that."

"How'd you know that?"

"I had a sense it would be a good job for me. I like people, and I like buying things."

"Did you ever have an interest in any other field or industry?"

"No, not really," he said.

"What would you say motivates you, gets you up in the morning?"

"You know, doing my job well. Being successful. Making my clients happy."

To grow up at work or to be a leader, however, that's not enough.

Leaders have a responsibility to have a high degree of self-awareness. It's not a nice-to-have leadership competence; it's a must-have. When we have a better understanding of who we are, we become more relatable to the people around us and can begin to build genuinely trusting relationships. By doing so, we become better leaders; people will be prepared to join us in facing greater challenges. We can motivate and inspire people more effectively not just by saying the right words but by playing the right "music," engaging with people emotionally rather than by delivering a prepared script. Self-awareness also means we have a realistic and accurate sense of how others perceive us.

Because Dennis didn't really know himself or wasn't comfortable with himself, he wasn't able to share himself with others. And to them, it seemed like there wasn't very much to get to know.

Drawing on my own experience

Given my Gestalt-oriented coaching work, I am in the habit of using myself as an instrument. I decided to try to understand Dennis and help him understand himself by examining my own experience when working with him. If I'm clear about my experience sitting with a client, it usually points them to something in themselves or in how others experience them.

(The big disclaimer here is that coaches, like therapists, need to be careful in conflating their experience of a client with their own *countertransference*, which is when a coach's unresolved emotional experiences get triggered by a client. If one's countertransference is triggered, then it's work for the coach/therapist, not the client. I was clear that what I was experiencing with Dennis was less about me, and more about him and his relationships.)

As I sat with Dennis, I noticed that I felt a combination of boredom, flatness, and sadness in his presence. I started to wonder whether a few of the Gestalt interruptions in contact were present in him, namely, deflection and egotism—both of which are discussed in other chapters of this book—since they are consistent with what I was experiencing.

It felt to me that Dennis had developed a habitual way of deflecting anything too vulnerable or emotional in himself in the presence of others. By keeping things on the level of the false self, he kept interactions safe, but they lacked substance or truth. His smile was constant, and it started to make me wonder what led him to smile so hard in nearly every interaction. What was the other feeling (usually the opposite of smiling) that he was trying to avoid?

Dennis was also likely experiencing egotism in the way he related to others, especially those whom he didn't think he needed to please. His way of relating had almost everything to do with him looking good, including, paradoxically, when he was providing great client service to others. But it always came back to him. Meanwhile, he seemed to have little interest in forming authentic relationships with his colleagues. His egotism might not have been as barbed as others, but it was getting in the way of true relationships forming.

Dennis had chosen to project a kind of hologram of himself to the world—his false self—as a way of avoiding any true contact. It was more than a lack of empathy; he was defining himself in one-dimensional ways—as smart or ambitious or successful and little more. Dennis figured this was fine for him, for his clients, and for his coworkers.

Except, of course, that it was not fine. While Dennis's clients did not expect to get to know the real Dennis—the professional Dennis was all they needed to know, it was different for Dennis's direct reports and peers. They expected to see a real version of Dennis and to be able to relate to him. The absence of this genuine relationship had led to a deep level of distrust among his colleagues—something Dennis had remained completely unaware of.

This serious lack of awareness of other people's perceptions suggested to me that there was indeed a vulnerability here. I started to wonder whether Dennis was protecting himself in some way.

In coaching, and in therapy, a good starting point is to get in touch with ourselves and our experiences. "What are you feeling right now?" is often a good question.

It was not a question that Dennis seemed to have asked himself very often. For a long time, when I posed the question to him, the answer seemed to be only that he was feeling blank, confused, and a little scared.

Looking within and beyond

Eventually, I decided to share my firsthand experience of Dennis with him. It can feel terrible in the moment to do this with a client, and yet I often hit pay dirt.

By our fourth session, Dennis and I had built some rapport, however superficial. And, as I struggled to stay engaged with our chit chat, I knew I had to take a chance.

"Dennis, do you mind if I share my experience of sitting here with you?"

"Sure, OK," he said, looking a little confused.

This wasn't going to be easy.

"Dennis, I noticed in this conversation and the last few that I'm actually drifting off a bit," I said. "I'm feeling a little distracted and even a bit bored. I don't say that to hurt your feelings, but I offer that because I consider it useful information. I don't usually feel bored with clients, so it makes me wonder what is going on for you and how you are affected hearing that from me."

Usually quick with his responses, this time Dennis paused. I couldn't tell if he was startled or just sobered.

"No one's ever told me that before. Uh, maybe that's why I have trouble dating," he said, trying to make a joke.

I smiled and thought, *now we might be getting to something real.*

"I don't like the idea that you're bored while I'm talking," he said. "And I'm not sure what to do about that."

"I'm glad to hear that. I'm curious too and also really thankful you heard what I said with openness," I said. "That's a big first step, and I'm going to take a guess that what's happening here between us may actually give us some insights about what is happening between you and your staff at work. Do you think that's a possibility?"

"Maybe," he said. Maybe. That's when the work begins.

Not long after this, as he was sharing a family memory with me, Dennis mentioned something about his brother. I was confused, since I recalled that Dennis was an only child.

"Your brother?" I asked.

Dennis paused.

"Oh," he said softly. "There's something I need to tell you. I had a brother. His name was James, and he was three years older than me. He was killed when I was ten years old, in a car accident. He was coming back from a basketball game played in another town, and another car struck the one he was in, driven by his friend's mom. His death was a great shock and a tremendous loss for our family. I'm not sure we ever got over it."

I stopped, I paused, I breathed. I slowed down.

"Wow," I shared. "I'm so sorry to hear about your brother. This sounds incredibly painful for you and for your parents. Do you know why you never told me before now?"

Dennis looked down. "I don't know. It's in the past, and I don't like to think about it too much."

It became increasingly clear that Dennis had never been able to deal properly with the trauma and grief of losing his brother. Ten years old was young enough to have been devasted by the pain, but old enough not to have been able to allow himself to grieve as much as he would have liked or as much as he deserved. Instead, he had focused on putting on a brave face. It seemed that his parents had too.

Together, we began the process of working with his unresolved grief, including his feelings of sadness, anger, and a familiar numbness. In theoretical terms, his unprocessed grief was an "unfinished Gestalt," a situation or dynamic in need of resolution. I started to believe that the lack of closure was preventing Dennis from striking a healthy relationship between himself and his environment, cutting him off from his own feelings and from relating deeply to others.

The avoidance of his grief and his tendency toward deflection had served Dennis as a child, and I didn't fault him for developing this as his coping mechanism. What was also true was that the coping mechanism of deflection had become chronic and habitual throughout the rest of his life.

Dennis needed to understand that it was entirely right to feel compassion for the poor lost little boy who was his younger self—to reach out to him with love and affection and allow himself to work through the grief that he had not allowed himself to experience at the time. For this reason, I referred Dennis to a psychotherapist who specialized in working with unresolved grief. It was my sense that this work would serve Dennis greatly and would deepen our coaching work together.

A reappraisal

As he began to work through this unresolved pain from his past, Dennis slowly became more real to me, more relatable, and less like a cardboard cutout of himself. The walls began to come down. He allowed himself to be "seen" by me and to be a little vulnerable, step by step.

Dennis didn't have an answer for every question anymore, no more dinner party repartee. He wasn't trying to entertain me, and sometimes he got teary when he spoke about his parents and being the first family member to be born in this country. He was less animated and more vulnerable. Previously polished and put together in ties and cufflinks, he began coming to our sessions in sweats and baseball caps. He felt freer to be himself.

As we explored his new feelings, he admitted that he had been dimly aware of the nature of his relationships with other people.

"I often feel I don't know what I want. And I don't know how to connect with other people."

"Is there something you are afraid of?"

"I'm not sure. What if people don't like me? What if they *do* like me, and then I might lose them?" he replied, his voice cracking a bit.

"I've really not been able to look back after James died. It's just too painful. And I guess I felt that I didn't want to get too close to anybody else because then I opened myself up to the possibility of losing them and facing more pain.

"It's not that I don't want to be close to anyone else," he said. "It's just ... I didn't ..."

We both sat in silence for a while.

Unresolved grief (and trauma and loss) have a sneaky way of showing up for our attention in changed and attenuated forms. Whenever memory of his grief peeked around the corner at Dennis, he would panic and shut down.

As he took the time to explore himself and his own feelings about the grief in his past and his present reaction to it, Dennis became aware of the possibility of a new relationship to the people around him and to the world at large.

He had persuaded himself that he was happy as a bachelor—so few complications! Now that he was reappraising his relationships at work, he began also to reappraise his entire approach to life. The coping mechanisms that he had used to deal with the world when he was uncomfortable in his own skin slowly began to fall away. He began to understand that he had constructed, crafted, and projected a false self, one based on an idea of who he could or should be. Of course, this false self had lacked truthfulness or depth.

Now, as Dennis began to feel less one-dimensional and more of a real person, he began to feel that he wanted more from life and to wonder if he did want to let other people into that life.

"Until now, I felt like I did what I was supposed to do in life, but something has felt a little empty," he said. "I haven't had that much in my life besides my work for several years, and I'm starting to realize that maybe I have been afraid to get close to people. But that has a price, right? And is it really what I want?"

I liked this Dennis. He didn't bore me at all.

Opening up

This whole process, as you would imagine, was not a fast or an easy one for Dennis. Our coaching sessions went on for almost a year. Dismantling the mechanisms that he had used to cope with grief reopened deep wounds. He continued to work with a psychotherapist during this time too.

Dennis went through a painful and belated grieving process. He told me that he had found himself crying himself to sleep and waking up in the morning to a jolt of pain as the reality of James's death came back to him anew. He also told me that he was learning to accept and cope with it, rather than throwing up walls to shut the pain away.

We discussed his identity as a second-generation American from an immigrant family unfamiliar with therapy, self-disclosure, and vulnerability. We also reflected on how counter-cultural it was for him to be doing this important introspective work, a process that his elderly parents would likely be unable or uninclined to do themselves.

As he learned to be more tender toward himself and the younger part of him that had experienced the loss of his brother, he learned to like himself more. With time, he could look back at his younger self with more understanding and affection, rather than as a place that was too painful to revisit. He became more likeable. The people around him began to feel they could relate to him more. He stopped showing up at work as a one-dimensional person and began becoming a leader who could demonstrate more self-awareness, honesty, and realness.

Dennis slowly began to let people into his life, and they started to feel like they could relate to him better as he grew more comfortable sharing anecdotes, stories, and little bits of personal history that allowed them to get to know his triumphs, his errors, and things he had learned along the way. He started to spend time with his colleagues outside of the office and to reinvigorate his social life. He even thought about looking for a serious relationship, ending a habit of keeping others at an emotional distance.

Real authenticity always has a spontaneous quality to it. It's born out of the moment, not out of some preformed idea of ourselves, our roles, and others. Now that Dennis was no longer performing to a script in his head about who he was, how he should act, and what he should say, he became more authentic and real to his colleagues.

As we concluded our coaching work together, Dennis remarked that he felt different inside and outside. He was more aware of his feelings and less guided by who he thought he *should* be.

He took an interest in forming more meaningful relationships at work, particularly with his staff. In his one-on-one meetings with his direct reports, he began to ask questions about how they were doing and what challenges they were facing in their work, along with their career interests.

At first, his staff was confused by these questions. I encouraged Dennis to share with them that he was practicing new management habits to grow as a leader, which demonstrated his sincerity—another way we can build trust with others.

As Dennis continued to make these efforts, his staff began to believe that he genuinely wished to grow, and they started to share more with him. On a recent 360 assessment, taken two years after my interviews were conducted, his staff indicated that they felt Dennis had developed as a manager and as a leader, and they reported that they trusted him more. The staff also remarked on his sincere willingness to be more open and real, and this made him not only more compelling as a colleague, but also as a human being.

► **REFLECTIONS** ◄

- How well do the people around me know me?

- How much do I allow them to know me?

- How well do I know myself?

- Is there any unresolved grief, pain, or trauma from my past or present that I am "managing" each day so that I don't feel it?

- Is that grief, pain, or trauma expressing itself in other ways?

- How do I show up to people in different contexts? Do my friends know me as the same person my colleagues know? Am I hiding or "shape-shifting" in any of these spaces?

- What kinds of relationships do I want to cultivate at work?

► **PRACTICES** ◄

- Work on showing up in new ways and not defaulting to your old way of being.

- When someone reaches out to you for advice or guidance, seize the opportunity. Make sure you are genuinely there for them.

- Work with a therapist or coach to deal with any unresolved trauma or grief in your past; it is almost impossible to do this on your own.

► EXPERIMENTS ◄

These are best done when followed by journaling or reflection to understand and "seal" the experience.

- Try sharing more about yourself (including your thoughts and feelings) with others than you have ever dreamed of doing before.

- Ask others how they feel about you, your working relationship, and what they need from you.

- Actively build trust by communicating with more warmth and openness toward others.

Chapter 9

I'm Successful, but I Have No Life

ALISON CARRIED HERSELF WITH EXCEPTIONAL confidence and maturity for a twenty-eight-year-old. She was five foot nine and regularly wore elegant skirt suits along with modern, asymmetrical blouses. She usually wore heels, in which she walked with ease, and had her thick hair up, usually with an elegant barrette. Her chunky glasses added hipness and also helped her look a few years older.

In fact, most of Alison's peers at the New York public relations firm where she worked were in their late forties and early fifties. Alison was very able and astute, and that talent had been recognized early on by the head of her division. Within a year of being hired by the firm, she had been earmarked for the executive suite.

However, what became clear to me almost as soon as Alison walked through the door was that she was tired. More than tired. Exhausted. Despite her style, sophistication, and obvious intelligence, she gave the distinct impression of someone who was emotionally flat. Joyless, almost.

The road to burnout

Beyond Alison's tremendous sense of style and maturity, I discovered her background was from a white working-class family, but she had won a scholarship to a prominent university in the Midwest, where she excelled. After graduation, she took up her post at the public relations firm in New York City, and by the time I met her, she was already considered a successor to one of the top executives in the firm.

"I've been working seventy-hour weeks since I got my job," Alison said. "I feel like I've been in fifth gear for years. Don't get me wrong. I love my job, I know I'm good at it, but it's all I do. There are so many things I just never get to."

Despite once having had a thriving social life, she had lost touch with almost all of her friends. Alison spent a lot of time in planes and airports flying to client sites. She would frequently wake in hotels and have to take a few minutes to remember which city she was in. Her college roommate had recently gotten married, and Alison had missed it when she was called in over the weekend to handle a new client presentation. Weddings, holidays, christenings, and all sorts of parties and get-togethers had all been sacrificed on the altar of work.

"My sister and her husband live three blocks away in the city, but I never see them," she told me. "I feel so guilty about that. But I'm doing OK, all things considered. I'm working more than I've ever worked in my life, and I know I'm not alone in this. The whole team is moving fast."

She turned to me, her face a question mark. "I guess this is just what it takes right now?"

Alison's firm was in the throes of restructuring, and the entire management team was given executive coaches to help them and their subordinates through a wide-ranging corporate transformation. In itself, this didn't present Alison with any particular challenges. But as we talked, the picture that emerged was of someone who no longer knew what she wanted.

What I thought I wanted

"Do you know how much I wanted a job like the one I have?" Alison asked me, even though it seemed like she was actually asking herself.

"I should feel lucky to have it. All of my friends in college can't believe how far I've come, so fast. I'm already in meetings with the CEO."

As she spoke, she didn't look particularly happy.

"I don't know. I just don't know what's going on with me," she said, running her fingers through her hair and looking like she was on the verge of tears.

As the session progressed, Alison told me how she had experienced a health scare just a week before our meeting. Returning to New York from a conference in Chicago on an early morning flight, Alison experienced crippling stomach pain, so bad that she ended up in the emergency room. Despite keeping her in the hospital for three days and running numerous tests, the doctors could not get to the bottom of what was wrong. It had happened twice in the preceding three months.

This is something else I've noticed with corporate warriors. They are very resistant to admitting to depression or anxiety and will instead somaticize their emotional and psychological stresses. By somaticize, I mean that their bodies manifest physical symptoms that are most likely symptoms of emotional distress. I'm not saying that Alison's ailments were imagined, rather that the breakneck pace at which she was living her life was clearly compromising her immune system in some way.

The other key factor in all of this was that Alison wanted to be a mother. Moreover, despite her lifestyle, she had managed by some miracle to carve out a stable, loving relationship. The fact that her partner, another corporate warrior, worked in the same firm was central to the relationship's functioning. He, too, was in favor of having a child.

"Besides having a successful career like this one, becoming a mom has always been my dream," Alison said, looking wistful.

"A mom?" I asked.

"More than anything."

Motherhood would become a kind of north star for Alison in the months to come, guiding her toward the changes that needed to be made and also serving as a reminder of the gaps between the life Alison wanted and the one she had.

Workaholism's effect on leadership

It was also interesting to see how Alison's workaholism affected her leadership within the organization. You would think that being this committed to work would serve as an advantage in guiding and mentoring staff, but the opposite was actually true.

In an effort not to overwork her staff, she found herself taking on part of their work—a dynamic that only served to exacerbate what had already been occurring in her own job. She took client calls late into the night and often woke up early each morning to be available for calls starting at 6 a.m. to accommodate clients based in Europe.

For a lot of leaders, the pacesetting becomes normalized. Some are addicted to work, I believe, and the addiction enables them to ignore parts of their life that aren't working. This dynamic often perpetuates itself, but ultimately, it's not good for anyone. Life isn't just about work. (Even though work is important to life.)

Working at a frenetic pace has a cost on leaders, the people who work for them, and on the climate of the organizations where they lead. The author of the seminal book *Emotional Intelligence*, Daniel Goleman calls this a "pace-setting" leadership style, and it is one that is best used sparingly and usually only in a temporary crisis since it can be exhausting and unsustainable over time.

Leaders must pay close attention to the explicit and implicit messages they send to the people who work for them. Even if a leader urges people to stop working at 5 p.m., but she is consistently sending emails out late at night, it sends a mixed message. And our actions speak loudest of all.

Leaders must ask themselves what kind of work climate they want to create, and they must be willing to have their actions reflect their aspirations.

In Alison's case, she wasn't explicit about telling her direct reports that they had to work as much as she did to be successful. Yet we can imagine they easily could have made that inference, even if she didn't want them to come to that conclusion.

Her frenetic pace had already driven one promising young executive out of the organization. In her exit interview, she explained that she was leaving because she could not keep up. "If that's what it means to be successful here," she said, "then I'm out."

I didn't have to ask Alison to know the answer to this question: "How's all of this working for you?"

Finding our inner voice

Good coaching is assisted self-discovery without judgment. My role is to create the right conditions for introspection and help clients like Alison slow down sufficiently to peel back the layers and see what's going on more clearly.

In his book *Excellent Sheep*, William Deresiewicz, then a professor at Yale University, observed that while those who graduate from exclusive universities like Ivy League institutions may be exceptionally bright, they are surprisingly unable to handle the bigger questions of life. They struggle to think critically and creatively. They don't know themselves and lack a clear sense of purpose. Many of these young people are products of high-achieving families who condition their children to aspire to a certain breed of success, which is in turn defined by a particular set of grades, a particular set of schools, a particular income bracket, and a particular zip code.

In Adult Development Theory, these people are locked in "socialized" rather than "self-authoring mind" forms of consciousness. Their ideas, values, and beliefs are untainted by introspection or scrutiny; instead, they are informed by what they think success means from a societal lens.

In Gestalt language, this is called "introjection," the unconscious process of adopting and living out beliefs, values, and ideas inculcated by upbringing. These things are absorbed unthinkingly to the point where they become part of what we are, and it should be said, they're not all bad. Our parents have transmitted the need to be responsible, to be kind, to treat people with respect. But it rarely stops there. We have also introjected a range of ideas that end up guiding our decision-making and, frequently, running the show.

The antidote lies in the practice of finding one's own inner voice. The beliefs and values that we absorb in childhood can be overpowering to the point that we follow them to the detriment of our own health and happiness. This kind of introspection, achieved through finding one's inner voice, allows for a life that is whole and more satisfying. Our lives outside of work can buffer us in our work.

Alison had decided at a young age that to be successful in her adult life, to achieve a certain kind of lifestyle, she would have to put on the suit, put on the pearls, get out there, work hard—and not stop.

"What do you think of your lifestyle? Is it working for you?" I asked.

"Not so much," she said. "I wanted a career like this one, and when I look at other successful leaders in the firm, this is how they live, too. My parents taught me to work very hard, and they keep reminding me that I should feel lucky to have achieved what I have. To have a job, to be paid so well. I'm sure they're right."

But she didn't look so sure. She looked distracted again, like she was there with me but somewhere else at the same time.

Despite or perhaps because of her success, Alison's parents were very fearful of her leaving her job and continually reminded her what a good job it was and how important it was to be paid well. There was a layer of fear inherited from her parents' experience of the world and underlying her motivations in all of this.

The other thing to point out here is that workaholism—or workism, as I've been hearing it termed recently—is one of the most socially acceptable addictions. I meet clients who are so busy, they're spinning. They're often ten to fifteen minutes late for our phone call, and they're frequently a little behind in their work. You can feel the stress rising from them like smoke.

The reality is that when you do this, you're defining yourself through something you're *doing* as opposed to something that you *are*, that you're being. And there are secondary benefits associated with overwork that you can't ignore. If all of your time and energy is directed into your career, the subtle payoff is that you don't have to look at the parts of your life that are not working. Alison had become adept, as many people do, at shutting away these uncomfortable feelings in a drawer. And it is this that creates the pain, the flatness, the illness. Because you can't just squash one feeling, you tend to squash them all. Discomfort and malaise are squeezed out, but so, too, is joy.

Alison wasn't exactly oblivious to the clues she was receiving about the disconnect between the life she was living and the one she wanted. She never saw her sister. She said she wanted to cook but ended up eating cereal on the couch at eleven at night. There were the hospitalizations and her unequivocal yearning for motherhood.

And she was simply exhausted. So many of the other Alisons I've met go flat out all week and can do nothing at the weekend but recover. At some point, they realize that it simply isn't enough. It's not a full life. Change happens, but really in my experience, it often doesn't come until you have hit some sort of rock bottom.

Start by feeling our feelings

In our coaching work together, my aim was to slow everything down, to try to help Alison feel what she was actually *feeling*, to see where she was in her life, and to explore where she wanted to be. In a sense, her overwork had served as a *defense* against feeling her actual feelings.

This is how defenses work. They defend us from something more painful underneath. But to get to the other side—to actually *transform* ourselves—we must be willing to move past our defenses to see what painful feelings we are trying to avoid.

"What are you feeling right now?" I asked her during one of our sessions.

"Not much. I feel fine," she said.

"Would you say that you feel some flatness, some numbness?"

"Yeah, that feels accurate," she said. "Some flatness, a sense of not-feeling-ness."

I paused, and we sat together in silence for a few moments.

As I looked at Alison, I didn't feel numb myself; I felt a sense of despair. I decided it was time to take a chance. I shared with Alison my own experience of being with her.

"When I look at you, Alison, and I listen to you, I feel sad. I wonder if you're aware of any sadness?" I said. "Are you aware of any shifts in sensation or energy when I say this to you?"

At first, all Alison could feel was numbness. In essence, what she felt was an absence of feeling.

I asked Alison to sit with the numbness. There was nothing wrong with it, I suggested. Numbness is not an uncommon experience for clients. In my observation, it can either be a symptom of depression, or it can serve as a way to avoid a deeper feeling that is more raw, painful, and vulnerable.

Alison paused and said she felt sad that I felt sad. I asked her to breathe more deeply. With some more moments of shared silence, I could see that she was starting to tear up, her sadness was starting to emerge—slowly, softly.

Indeed, Alison soon began to sense other feelings that were present for her too. Many of Alison's feelings were, in fact, dimensions of grief. I asked her to put words around these feelings for me.

"The truth is, I'm not happy. I feel like I've done all the things, all the things I was supposed to for a happy, successful career, but this just isn't working out the way I hoped," she said. "I'm mad at this firm, I'm mad at everyone running around so fast, expecting that the rest of us will do the same. I think I'm also mad at myself."

With the gift of time—time she had not made for a long while, if ever—Alison and I explored the variety of feelings she had unearthed. Exhaustion was the first and most obvious layer; it's what she presented with first, and it was the thing that was most evident. Alison was bone tired, and her overwork had led to a life consisting of work, rest, work, rest, on repeat. This was not sustainable, and she began to feel that truth more and more.

Alison felt sad that her twenties had basically been devoted to being a worker, a doer, a performer. She had very little time to play and to pursue any of her other interests, which included creative writing. With time to reflect, Alison felt sad by the lack of joy and delight that she wanted more of in her day-to-day life.

"I've missed having interests outside of work," she said. "Did you know that before I joined this firm, I planned on being a writer? I imagined myself writing fiction or poetry or being a journalist. I have missed writing a lot. It always helps me feel closer to myself."

And beyond the sadness? We found resentment and anger. As previously discussed, when we are confluent with our environment—when we go along with others, despite feeling differently—over time, we tend to feel resentment (or guilt, or both). Being confluent with a corporate system of warriorship was no longer something Alison wanted to enact, and by feeling resentment, she could see how she had actually been betraying herself and her needs as a result.

Finally, by feeling angry, Alison grew resolute about making some new decisions. Every emotion has wisdom within it, and the wisdom within anger is that it usually points us to injustice in our lives. While we could argue that Alison's boss was being unjust in his expectations of her, the truth was that *Alison herself* was being unjust in what she expected of herself. She also started to question a corporate culture that didn't seem to value anything beyond how she performed.

What do you want from your one wild and precious life?

As Alison began to feel her feelings, our progress naturally led to another classic coaching question. To quote one of my favorite poets, Mary Oliver: "Tell me, what is it you plan to do with your one wild and precious life?"

This is a question we should all ask ourselves: What does success mean to you?

Take a world-famous and wealthy author in my extended social network. This person has sold millions of books but has also had three painful divorces and none of his adult children speak to him. Compare him to someone else who has never been published, has had a so-so career, but has a loving family and feels very connected to his community. Which one is more "successful"? It depends on what that word means to you. And it very well may change over time and with greater emotional honesty.

One of my all-time favorite quotes is by Goethe: "Once you trust yourself, you will know how to live." I've always found that to be a gorgeous instruction for life. I think it may be true for leadership as well.

Many leaders, who have been conditioned to be overachievers, don't usually stop for too long to ask how their life, their *whole* life, is working for them. They are so focused on performance and achievement that it can often take a crisis to get them to stop, take stock, and make some different choices.

With Alison, a certain compulsive tendency emerged over time, one clearly manifested in her workaholism. She was like a frog in boiling water who cannot understand what is happening but knows that things are getting increasingly uncomfortable.

Connecting back to our values

"OK, you want to have a child," I said to Alison. She nodded.

I continued, "You're in your late twenties, and your partner wants to start a family too. Great."

Her eyes widened and she smiled. Talking about having a child always brought a brightened and more tender look to her face.

"How do you think your current lifestyle could support having a child?" I asked. "How do you see those two things coexisting?"

Alison thought for a minute.

"I have no idea how I would do that," she said. "Some days I have to take calls at 6 a.m., and the same day I could have another call at 10 p.m. because of the time zone differences. Plus, I take about thirty flights a year."

"How do you feel physically?" I asked.

While Alison was usually dressed up in formal business attire, today we were on a video call. She was calling from a hotel in Orlando where she had attended a conference. Her hair was up in a ponytail and she was wearing a hoodie and no makeup. She looked younger to me and more fatigued than ever. It looked like she had been crying.

"I feel like a wreck," she said. "I'm tired, and I'm still having those headaches I told you about. I'm just shattered. I can't imagine myself pregnant. It just wouldn't be possible."

"But is this something you want?" I gently pressed her.

She didn't hesitate.

"More than anything."

What does success mean to me?

A week later, Alison was back in my office. She had just been offered a promotion.

The role of global head of Communications had come vacant following a reshuffle. This was exactly the job she had targeted eight years earlier when she had joined the firm. She wasn't even thirty and someone was dangling the holy grail in front of her. The new role would require relocation to London, but it came with all the trappings of corporate royalty: an apartment, a car and driver, a fat expense account, and more.

"My parents are ecstatic," she said, "They're already looking at flights to London. My boss says it's a once-in-a-lifetime opportunity, and he's right. It is."

"What do you think?"

"Excuse me?" She looked confused and squinted at me, as if she had trouble hearing me.

"What do *you* think about this offer? Do you want it?"

"I'd be crazy to turn it down."

"Yes, but do you want it?" I asked. "What do *you* want?"

This was the crux of it all—to penetrate the crust of acquired values and beliefs (introjects) that had guided Alison to this point in her life, that were unconsciously directing her decision-making. Yes, she had experienced great success, but it was an exceptionally narrow form of success that would not admit friendships or hobbies or health or motherhood. And even as she told me about this once-in-a-lifetime opportunity, there was no joy in her voice, no excitement. She was, in fact, on the point of tears.

The antidote lies in the practice of finding, and listening to, your inner voice. The beliefs and values that we absorb in childhood can be overpowering, to the point that we will follow them single-mindedly, even to the detriment of our own health. The coaching process draws attention to this dynamic and seeks to amplify the faint voice of the higher Self, so that person can say, "I recognize *my* values, *my* beliefs." As I've pointed out before, the real work here tends to happen between sessions, which are there to catalyze the process of self-discovery.

In our sessions, I sought to amplify the faint voice of Alison's Self so that she could recognize *her* values and *her* beliefs. Outside of our work, Alison kept a good journal, and that activity proved helpful in drawing out her voice and clarifying what it was that she wanted.

It was full of poetry and stream-of-consciousness prose, the kind of writing that made me think about the untapped market of businesspeople creating art on the road. Articulating her desires and practicing her passion allowed Alison to clear her head and answer truthfully these questions: What does success mean to me? What is important to me? What do I want from life?

Learning to respect our needs

Alison didn't take the job, and her parents felt concerned and afraid. They didn't understand her decision at all, which caused Alison to second-guess herself.

"Do you think I'm making a mistake?" she asked me. "I hate disappointing them."

It represented one of the bigger steps of psychological "individuation," or a step toward self-authorship, that she had taken in her life. While her parents were operating from a socialized mind perspective, one of scarcity, I could step in to affirm her.

"I don't think you're making a mistake, and you may be disappointing your parents. Both things can be true at the same time," I said. "As I've listened to you now for months and seen your health issues, I feel your decision was born out of a lot of consideration for your own values and what you want. It feels very consistent, though that may be hard for your parents to understand."

She softened. Growing up at work sometimes means actually stepping away from our work, from what our manager wants from us, and from what our parents want from us—and turning toward what we want out of our lives.

Instead, Alison began asking the kinds of questions she had never asked herself before. Do I really need to travel for that meeting? Is my input really necessary on that call tonight? In subsequent sessions, we explored the possibility of finding work elsewhere, of discovering new ways of moving down from fifth gear to fourth. Maybe even third.

In the end, she chose to remain working with the same firm, albeit on a radically altered basis and in a new, less high-visibility role. She stopped working at 6 p.m., shopped for fresh food, and began cooking more—often with her sister. Slowly, she began to create boundaries to protect her personal life.

Four years have passed, and Alison works mostly virtually now—a habit that worked especially well during the COVID-19 pandemic. She brings her young son (yes, her son) to soccer on Tuesday afternoons and wears a lot more yoga pants than she used to.

By defining her success more holistically, Alison learned to set a different kind of example for her direct reports and no longer engaged in such a steady pace of overwork. She retained high expectations both of her own work and that of her staff, but she also demonstrated support and care when members of her team needed time off.

She recognized the difference between marching to someone else's tune and finding her own voice. Alison finally understood the power of greater self-care and balance and no longer defined success as narrowly as she once had. This allowed her to coach her own staff with greater empathy.

Alison put her lifestyle on a more sustainable footing, and because she was able to dodge the inevitable burnout, the firm was able to retain her skills. In fact, of the executive team members who initially received coaching, she is the only one who remains on staff today. Looking back, it's clear to her that it would not have been humanly possible to continue to operate as she had been and at the same time achieve her personal goals.

"This is the life I wanted, but I realize that I had to choose it," she said. "I had to make it happen."

► **REFLECTIONS** ◄

- How do I define success for myself?

- Whose definition am I using when I think about success? How much of the definition has been explicitly or implicitly derived from others' definitions—especially from my family of origin?

- When have I felt most fulfilled?

- Am I making decisions out of fear or out of trust?

- As a leader, what kind of work climate do I want to create for others? Am I living that way myself? What mixed messages might I be sending?

► **PRACTICES** ◄

- Be honest with yourself by assessing how satisfied you are across different areas of your life (e.g., friendships, hobbies, personal growth, health, career, etc.) and talk to a friend or coach about your scores. (This is also called the "Wheel of Life" exercise.) Are your scores OK with you? Is this the life you want to live? What scores do you wish were higher? What would that life look like?

- What trade-offs are you making? Are you OK with them? What tweaks could you make to be more in balance with yourself?

- Keep coming back to the question of what success means *to you*—not anyone else. Write down your own operating instructions for being happy.

- Write down the things that you like. Compare that list to how you're actually spending your time. Is there enough overlap for you?

▶   **EXPERIMENTS**   ◀

- Stop working an hour before you think you should.

- Do less and see what happens.

- Cook one dinner for yourself once a week.

- Take a class in one of your former hobbies.

- Block time on your calendar for yourself and notice whether you respect it or override it.

Chapter 10

I Have to Be Perfect

IF YOU WERE TO MEET Joy when I first did some years ago, I suspect that your initial reaction would have been to think how accomplished she seemed.

Joy had many of the hallmarks of what we usually consider success and extraordinary intelligence. A Black Caribbean-American woman in her mid-thirties, Joy was always impeccably dressed in jewel-toned suits and sported a lovely though infrequent smile. She had graduated a year early from one of the top public high schools in New York City, which she immediately followed by attending a prestigious college and then a top-tier law school.

Her impressive academic career was followed by a succession of increasingly high-powered jobs in various law firms, which led to her current senior role at a major partnership. Joy was not yet herself a partner in the firm, but it appeared that was the next step.

Her husband sounded equally impressive, with a senior role in

Marketing at a large pharmaceutical company, and they were thinking about starting a family.

It's true that, at the time, Joy came across as a rather serious person, without many smiles or laughs. She was determined, resolute, and intense—and she brought these qualities to everything she did.

People don't like working for me

Joy found me through a close friend who had attended one of my leadership classes. Based on her friend's recommendation, Joy was interested in working with me because I approached coaching through the lens of psychotherapy. She suspected she needed help both at work and in her personal life. For a person who had worked hard to cultivate a successful life, acknowledging she needed help was already a big step for her.

In the early stages of coaching or therapy, you get to hear about the obvious problems, the things that people experience that make them unhappy. It can take awhile—years, for some clients—to get to the bottom of what drives those experiences. And then it takes more time for the person to fully address those issues so that they can develop into a newer, happier, more fulfilled version of themselves.

In Joy's case, one "problem" was clear from the start. She had begun to realize that people at work (specifically, the junior associates in the firm) didn't like working with her. In fact, they disliked it so much that they were quitting their jobs and moving to competitive law firms. Joy had now lost a number of good people who had made it clear on their departure that they found themselves unable to work for her any longer.

Nothing, it seemed, was ever good enough for Joy. She was demanding, which was perhaps to be expected, but she also seemed to have a problem appreciating people's work. She would critique it harshly, often working over elements of their documents and briefings herself before she would allow them to be presented to a client.

Joy's staff were all clearly in awe of her intellect and her abilities but found it hard to relate to her personally. They expected to be driven hard and welcomed the high-intensity atmosphere of the firm. But they were finding that working for Joy was too unrewarding and too damaging to their self-esteem. And the loss of talented staff was beginning to become an issue with the partners of the firm. They hoped that Joy would eventually become a partner of the firm, but she needed to be able to retain young lawyers to make that possible.

On the face of it, this was what had driven Joy to seek help. But she also admitted that she was not entirely happy either.

She described feelings of tension and anxiety, a kind of ever-present sense of malaise that she couldn't quite put her finger on. Her marriage was good, she said. She and her husband bickered at times and they rarely had time for each other, all of which seemed normal given how much each of them worked.

"How happy are you? How satisfied are you, at work and at home?" I asked.

"I'm good," she said. Her tone had not changed from the hard-driving, fast-moving way she usually communicated.

As I got to know Joy, I started to wonder whether she might be suffering from a low-grade depression. She felt driven to do everything perfectly and was constantly reproaching herself for not living up to her own high standards. In this sense, her name served as a paradox.

Unfortunately, Joy did not have a lot of joy in her life.

Perfectionism

As our work together started, a hybrid of coaching and psychotherapy, significant aspects of Joy's upbringing and personal background began to emerge.

It became clear that praise from Joy's parents had always come as a result of her cleverness and of her successes at school and university. Success, young Joy had quickly learned, was the route to affirmation. If you did everything absolutely to the best of your abilities—perfectly, ideally—and were lauded by your teachers, then your parents would be delighted, and you could bask in their admiration and praise. But then, of course, they would just set a higher bar the next time.

Joy's parents were both highly accomplished professionals—her dad was a physician and her mom worked as an administrator at a university. They valued education, and they also had high expectations of Joy academically and professionally.

Sometime after Joy first started working with me, she told me she had recently spoken with her mother more about her childhood. By this stage, Joy was beginning to feel that her perfectionism might lie at the heart of her feeling of malaise. She had shared this idea with her mother, without suggesting that it was a major problem.

"Mom just smiled," Joy told me. "She affectionately reminded me that I had been a perfectionist ever since I had been a little girl. Whether I was in ballet class, taking violin lessons, or writing a book report, my mom told me that I was always focused on doing things perfectly, starting from a very young age."

Joy's mom told her that she could still see her daughter's furrowed brow as she practiced a song on the violin until there were no errors. She also recalled Joy practicing a speech in junior high until she had memorized every line.

"Mom was smiling and saying, 'Baby, this is just how you've always been! This is how our family is!'" Joy recalled. "She seemed to think it was wonderful. But I thought, my God! How long has this been going on? This has been a habit for my entire life—indeed, it seemed a family habit as well. *Where did all this come from?*"

Building our awareness

Gestalt-oriented work is fueled by building our awareness of what we experience and feel in the *here and now*, as well as an awareness of our patterns of behaving. The habits and creative adjustments we have acquired in the course of our lives can ease our emotional pain, but they can also get in the way of our emotional freedom and our ability to act with agency and accountability.

None of us exists in a vacuum; we are all connected to a complex web of social and environmental relationships that both constrain us and make us who we are. From here, our experiences emerge. And there is some rhyme and reason in how experiences arise, get responded to, and subside.

A central concept within Gestalt therapy is called the "cycle of experience." This starts out from the simplest of notions: that we become aware of our various needs—something as straightforward as hunger, sadness, or loneliness, or as complex as feelings of self-worth or personal fulfilment—and we realize that there is something that we can do about it. There are choices we can make about the steps we take to satisfy our needs and achieve our goals.

Over time there can be interruptions or blockages in our cycle of experience. Such interruptions prevent us from completing a cycle and achieving real satisfaction and closure. For instance, we may struggle to become aware of our need or impulse. Or we are aware of it but struggle to act on our insights. Or we act but fail to experience satisfaction. Because of the blockage, the energy that was meant to take us out into our environment to satisfy our needs is diverted inward, often resulting in neurotic mental patterns and sometimes, dysfunctional behavior.

If we can discover what is causing us to interrupt a cycle of experience, we can learn how to remove the blockage and redirect that energy out into the environment.

One of these interruptions is introjection—and that gets us back to Joy. As discussed in the previous chapter, introjection is when we guide our life by ideas or concepts—often in the form of "shoulds"—instead of responding to our life in an organic, spontaneous way.

In Joy's case, she had introjected, or internalized, the expectation of perfectionism for herself and others. It's unclear how much of this intro-jection was *taught* by her parents, but it certainly was "caught" in the ether. Over time, Joy's perfectionism hardened into a habit, one that pre-vented her from choosing alternative and preferable ways of responding to her environment.

"It's not that my parents told me I had to be perfect, but I could see that was pretty much the standard they lived by," she said. "My mom cleaned the kitchen to the point there were never any water spots on the counter, and my dad worked late into the night reading up on the latest medical journals. There was a sense in my family that things had to be done the right way, and that felt like my way, too."

The result was that Joy had one default mode: *I have this challenge and I have to complete it to perfection. And if I fail, my lovability and self-worth are at risk.* But this mode was not making her happy in herself. It's no fun being a perfectionist, and it was not making the people around her happy either.

Joy was often functioning within the socialized mind stage of Adult Development Theory, when our ideas and behaviors are driven by a nar-rative we have drawn from our family or from the society and culture in which we grew up. Instead of making our own choices and doing what is best for us in the here and now with a self-authoring mind, we fall back on the script we have absorbed from others in our early life. Our sense of worth is contingent on the judgment of others.

This way of operating works, up to a point—some people live their entire lives with a socialized mind—but at a cost. When we live exclu-sively in a mindset formed by our social conditioning, we abandon our capacity to choose our own direction in life. And this abandonment may come back to hurt us, especially if conditions change. Going along with what our environment supplies is fine, after all, while that environment is benign and supportive.

But what happens when the environment changes? What happens if the cost is too high?

A change in the environment

In Joy's case, she had found considerable personal reward in the praise heaped on her by her parents and teachers for her excellent schoolwork and academic achievements. If she simply paid attention to detail, went the extra mile, and delivered "perfect" work, she was rewarded with praise. This continued, happily, through her studies in college and at law school and into the early stages of her career. How could an employer have a problem with someone who is a perfectionist?

Attention to detail matters, in our own work and in the work of our direct reports. Successful people tend to be driven, and excellence is nothing to shy away from. Unlocking greatness in others and themselves is one of the talents of great leaders.

That said, leaders must be extra careful to distinguish between a pursuit of *excellence* and possessing the mindset and habits of *perfectionism*. When they are unaware of the perfectionism driving them, their behavior can throw staff into anxiety, fear, and distress, causing toxic cultures where the fear to make mistakes limits creative experimentation, initiative, or constructive disagreements.

The antidote to perfectionism is to first acknowledge that it stems from a deep-seated belief. Many believe that their perfectionism is vital and that, without it, they would be a failure or unlovable. Recognizing and acknowledging how much we are driven by perfectionism is an act of bravery. It's also where growing up and out of perfectionism starts.

The next step is to recognize the internal scripts that have led to this behavior and to consider and reflect on whether these scripts or this behavior truly serves you and the people around you. With time, we learn who we are beyond the perfectionism. We learn to be ourselves.

As we explored her upbringing, Joy found a deeper understanding of how her identity as a Black woman and her being a child of a highly accomplished family of Caribbean-American descent played into her perfectionism. Starting from an early age, her parents told her that as a Black person she'd have to work harder than everyone else around her, and that meant she couldn't make mistakes.

"Being Black meant that my parents made clear to me that things would probably be harder—in school and on the job. They told me that I was very smart and that counted for something. But they told me that as a Black woman I could not fail," she said. "I had to put 150 percent into everything I did, since systemic racism was still very real. They told me I had a responsibility to be exceptional and that would enable me to be successful."

Joy's parents and community had transmitted to her a set of social norms I often hear from BIPOC (Black, Indigenous, and people of color) individuals. Based on their lived experience of systemic racism in the United States, many BIPOC individuals have concluded that a non-white person must work extra hard to "earn" their place in educational and professional life. Joy had been raised to understand that there is little room for error, especially in high-profile settings. Indeed, it appeared that Joy's intellectual talents and serious temperament were simply reinforced through the cultural conditioning she received in being perfect to succeed. It was a *perfect* storm.

Until Joy became a manager, her perfectionism was even functional, as she readily stayed up for nights in a row, perfecting a brief for a senior partner in the firm. She did not come up against any resistance to how she operated until she had associates reporting to her who looked to her for direction, guidance, and support. Instead, the associates found only ego-deflating criticism, and they would eventually express their unhappiness by leaving Joy's team. At that point, Joy's worldview was challenged, and she became anxious.

This was familiar territory.

As Gestalt therapists Erving and Miriam Polster write in *Gestalt Therapy Integrated*, "The person who has swallowed whole the values of his parents, his school, and his society requires life to continue as before. When the world around him changes, he is fair game for anxiety and defensiveness . . . Even when the introjection is successfully accomplished, that is, when it is consistent with the actual world he lives in, he still pays a high price because he has given up his sense of free choice in life."

Perfectionism is a bully

The most significant step toward personal growth is to reach an awareness of the core beliefs and assumptions that are driving our experience of life. In Joy's case it was the belief, internalized from her early life experiences, family upbringing, and systemic racism that reward would come from being perfect and from delivering perfect work.

Joy built her identity around this idea of perfectionism—an identity that had seeped into how she actually felt about herself. When we looked more closely, we also discovered that Joy had hooked perfectionism to her self-worth. *I have to be perfect. If I'm not perfect, I'm not loveable.*

Perfectionism is a bully. Perfectionism also doesn't leave much room for happiness or personal fulfillment. There is always something to be unhappy and unfulfilled about. *Have I done this well enough? Can I really stop here, or must I try harder?*

"It didn't occur to me that I also had to work to be liked by the people who work for me," she said.

She was no longer succeeding at work; she was starting to fail. With reflection, Joy was also starting to wonder whether her identity as a perfectionist was working for her.

"I'd like us to get curious about something," I said at our next session. "What's it like being you, being a perfectionist at work?"

"I can't let anything leave my desk that has my name on it without checking it a hundred times," she said. "I also stay up very late to make sure I produce."

"Are you having fun? Are you enjoying yourself?"

She looked confused and said, "What? What did you say?"

"Do you enjoy yourself?"

"Well, I don't know," she replied. "I never really quite thought about it in those terms. It's not really the point. The point is to be the best."

As we spoke, I was trying to poke at her belief system. Perfectionism is a type of compulsion, and people with a compulsive personality often tend to come off as tense. There's often an urgent drive and edge to their personalities, and I wanted her to understand this about herself and how she could be perceived by others.

"When you're talking to me, Joy, I'm not hearing much about your own fun, and I've been picking up on what kind of feels like tension to me, but maybe that's putting it too strongly," I said. "You're very driven, and I'm just wondering how this works for you?"

"My measure of excellence has been perfection, not happiness," she said, even as something began to occur to her.

Not only had she been making other people miserable, but she was starting to realize that she was miserable, too.

It might seem as if that would be the happy ending of the story. *I don't want to be a perfectionist anymore.* In reality, it's not as simple as that.

Question the bully to honor the person you are becoming

Joy's perfectionism came with significant personal rewards; it gave her a sense of superiority and it kept her away from a nagging sense of lack and emptiness. This had turned into a very real kind of addiction. Like any substance addict who avoids the unresolved issues in their life by keeping themselves partly numb, so Joy's perfectionism kept at bay her deeply rooted anxieties about whether she was leading her life well.

As Joy learned more about the origins of her perfectionism and the damage that it was inflicting on the people around her (and on her own well-being), she began to learn to listen to herself more. To honor the person that she was becoming and to individuate—to separate herself psychologically from the ideas she had absorbed as a child.

She also started to look at perfectionism's negative impact on her life and the lives of others around her. Perfectionism was a habit that held her anxiety temporarily at bay but created a tremendous amount of tension in its wake. And as we looked further, Joy came to realize that while perfectionism was a deep-seated habit, it wasn't *all of her*.

We've discussed having other voices in your head in other chapters, and that's what we discovered in Joy's head, once we did an inventory of sorts. There was the perfectionist—a very familiar and internalized voice—but there were other parts of her too. There was the part that was afraid of the perfectionist, that felt bullied. And there was the voice that longed for ease and yes, joy, more than perfection.

We got to know these voices within Joy, and we were able to identify that the perfectionist voice tended to retroflect or attack Joy on a regular basis if anything she did wasn't up to snuff. By isolating the retroflecting voice (based on a deeply held introject), Joy could see its origins, what she was trying to do, and the pain she created.

Indeed, most of the time when we attack ourselves, it comes from a much younger part that developed to do this (Freud would probably call it our superego). But that less mature consciousness usually oversimplifies things.

Joy's self-attack told her that if she wasn't perfect, the world would end and that she would be a failure. Thirty-something adult Joy was able to see that distorted belief for what it was and was able to question it.

When we begin to question the beliefs that have driven us unconsciously, we start having choices.

At the heart of her dawning new approach to life was the realization that she could live using a "learning mindset," an orientation toward life that assumes that everything is an opportunity for learning and growth.

Artists, in particular, understand that none of their work is ever "perfect." It may be very good, and they may be happy with it, but it is only the next stage on a journey to a perfection that they fully understand is unachievable. As the novelist Margaret Atwood put it, "If I waited for perfection, I would never write a word."

A learning mindset

Joy's perfectionism had naturally intruded into her personal life. House-work, shopping, planning vacations, decorating the apartment—all of these day-to-day tasks had been approached with meticulous planning and disconcerting rigor. A few years earlier, she had organized her best friend's wedding shower with her usual perfectionism. Even though she had executed the shower impeccably, Joy told me that she had been exhausted and sad and hardly enjoyed the event.

"The baby shower would have looked perfect on Instagram, but the truth is, I didn't have any fun," she said. "I was running around all morn-ing trying to make sure the centerpiece fit into my total vision, but that meant walking about ten city blocks with two dozen balloons because I couldn't get a taxi to pick me up. Why do I need it to be like this?"

We tried some simple experiments. First, I asked her to carry out some tasks in a deliberately imperfect way and see what happened. One way of doing this was to set time limits. At the end of the allo-cated time, she would have to abandon the task, regardless of its state of perfection.

I asked Joy to consider how she felt about the abandoned, imperfect tasks. How terrible were the consequences? Joy expected to feel a sense of abject failure because she had lost sight of where her self ended and the perfectionism began. Instead, she found the outcome was less apocalyptic than expected.

She also realized she had more energy when she was not pushing herself to produce perfect results. Next, I asked Joy to begin to see her team's "failures" as learning opportunities.

"Why don't you confide in them that you think you might have been too much of a perfectionist in the past, and you want to move beyond this?" I suggested.

Joy agreed to try. She also began to praise her team for their work and then to explore how aspects of their less-than-perfect work could be used improve things and develop them as professionals.

All of these activities and Joy's growing self-awareness began to allow a new Joy to emerge. She became kinder, gentler, and less self-critical, and her openness with her team made her instantly more approachable. Joy would always be a driven and committed leader, but her new approach meant that her team members could appreciate the challenge of working for someone as demanding as Joy, while feeling rewarded by her appreciation of their work and her positive suggestions for improvement.

Joy became, in their eyes, a more human, likeable leader to whom they could relate personally—someone who used mistakes and challenges as opportunities for learning and growth rather than as occasions for shame and blame. She made more room for humor and flexibility and was not as rigid.

I checked in with her manager, who said she had long admired Joy for her intellect and sharp legal mind. She said she had worried that might go away if the coaching was focused too heavily on Joy's people skills.

"But now, I realize that if Joy wants to become a partner, she needs to engage these associates," her boss told me. "I'm starting to notice how something is softening in how she is approaching her colleagues, and I feel encouraged to see such progress. I also heard from one of her associates that Joy is mentoring her team more than ever."

A lost childhood

There was one other aspect of Joy's early-acquired addiction to perfectionism. She had lost parts of her childhood.

The years that should have been spent playing in a joyful, unfettered, unstructured way had been constrained by an obsession with "success." Joy had never truly been able to simply have fun or mess about with no particular object in sight or standards to adhere to. *Everything* had to be carried out in an impressive way designed to elicit the reward of praise, the all-important "well done!"

Joy now wanted to rediscover that lost childhood. And she had the perfect opportunity: Joy and her husband had a baby. As their daughter grew, Joy was able to rediscover the *joy* of play. She started to look at parenting as a chance to be more fluid, creative, and open.

Joy told me about one moment when her own mother was playing with her new granddaughter. The toddler was having a delightful time fingerpainting. She didn't always keep the paint perfectly on the paper, nor was there any discernable composition. She was having fun. Joy's mother watched her granddaughter carefully as she painted, and offered her praise only when she made a shape that resembled a flower: *Good girl!*

"I said, 'Just let her play, Mom. It's not a test,'" Joy said.

She ruefully recognized the seeds of her own growing addiction to perfectionism: the drip feed of her mother's constant and well-intended reward for things achieved and done "successfully."

"I wasn't angry," Joy told me, "but I was a bit sad. It should be OK for your parents to tell you you've done something well. But for me, it became everything. I thought, 'This is what Mom and Dad and my teachers expect from me. This is what I have to do to be loved.' I tried to be perfect, and people told me I was brilliant and that was my route through life. I didn't realize it would make me unhappy or a difficult person. And now I see how it became too much. It began to consume who I am."

Learning to love ourselves

Perfectionism is not a natural state. "Find me a perfect leaf or a perfect tree," my spiritual teacher, Adyashanti, has said. Our lived experience as human beings is often messy and less than perfect—marked by trials, successes, obstacles, and failures. Perfectionism is an internal bully aimed at controlling our experience, and others. It's exhausting and it's rarely satisfied. It keeps us on an obsessive-compulsive loop of control. It is also lacking in tenderness, love, and acceptance.

Joy's growth was accelerated through our work together, which continued for another couple of years. Not only did she experiment with having more of a learning mindset with her staff, she tried to apply this mindset to herself as well.

When she threw a bridal shower for another friend, for instance, she approached the event primarily with the idea of making it fun and "good enough." She wanted to actually enjoy spending time with her friends, and she didn't need to be the perfect event planner. She noted that while the napkins might not have perfectly matched the balloons, and the chocolate cake she baked could have been less sweet, it was all good enough. She didn't go through her typical mental "post-mortem," criticizing herself and berating herself for her errors. Instead, she put up her feet, leaned back on the couch, sipped a glass of wine, and smiled. This was a huge accomplishment for Joy, and she celebrated it.

As Joy put it, our work together led her to no small feat: She learned to love herself more. She learned to be accepting of herself, which included her many talents but also her limitations and her humanity. She also realized that breaking the intergenerational legacy of perfectionism now had bigger implications. She was the daughter of proud perfectionists, and they had their own good reasons for being that way, but she didn't need to perpetuate that mindset. Joy did not want to be the mother of a perfectionist, nor did she want to uphold a practice associated with systemic racism where no one wins.

While she wanted her daughter to learn the beauty of pursuing and practicing her interests, she also wanted to show her the line between striving for excellence and achieving perfection. Her daughter continued to enjoy drawing as she grew older, and Joy's support of her daughter led to the creation of many lovely pieces of art.

"It may be a lifelong exercise for me to keep combatting my habit of perfectionism, and I know it's not easy for the people around me," she said. "But what motivates me the most is that I don't want to pass this habit on to my daughter. As a mom, I want to accept and love her exactly as she is, just as I'm learning to accept and love myself."

► REFLECTIONS ◄

- Am I a perfectionist? Even if I don't think so, have other people often given me this feedback?

- Do I tend to ignore this feedback? Do I not see it as being an issue?

- What is the payoff of being a perfectionist? Does it give me a sense of superiority? Am I effectively addicted to this behavior? What's the price of perfectionism on my life?

- Why do I often feel exasperated by the behavior of others? Is it really that they are not trying hard enough? Why do I get the urge to step in and do things better myself?

- How does being a perfectionist affect my relationships? Are there signs that people find me demanding and difficult? Am I OK with that?

- What would it mean to shift from a standard of perfectionism to a pursuit of excellence?

▶ PRACTICES ◀

What we are trying to achieve is a fuller awareness of how we behave, what is driving those behaviors, and how they affect those around us. These practices can help:

- Journaling: Write in a journal whenever you can.

  ○ Record the main things that you did that day. Was the amount of time and energy you devoted to each task appropriate?

  ○ Make notes on your interactions with other people. How do you feel they went? Did some of your conversations seem tense or difficult? What aspects of your own behavior may have caused that?

- Practice appreciation.

  ○ Start to view your interactions with other people as an act of generosity on their behalf. They have brought something to you. Be grateful, show your appreciation, and respond in a positive way.

  ○ If you think you should make a comment, praise the things that you find positive and offer guidance and useful suggestions as to how things might be improved.

- Learn to play.

  ○ Do something just for fun—anything that you genuinely enjoy doing.

- ○ Don't approach it as a learning experience or as practice; just mess around.

- ○ If you find yourself thinking *I must get better at this*, then stop and do something else. Go for a walk. Listen to some music. Do a jigsaw. Just play.

▶   **EXPERIMENTS**   ◀

Perfectionists fear that if they do anything less than perfectly, they will not be able to live with themselves and their self-esteem will take a terrible blow.

- Practice doing things imperfectly.

- Set yourself a time limit for any task. When your time is up, stop what you're doing and consider how you feel.

- Try telling your colleagues that you fear you may be a perfectionist and you want to approach things differently in the future.

- In your interactions at work, try using suggestive language: "What if we tried...?" "I wonder what would happen if we...?"

- Schedule a "playdate" for yourself—choose something your younger self would have enjoyed doing as a child.

Chapter 11

I'm Scared of My Boss

AT LEAST HALF A DOZEN times a year, I sit with clients who start by telling me about their boss. As they talk, I see their whole body tense up. They grow slightly smaller in the chair, and an unmistakable look of fear comes into their eyes. It's usually one of two things: Either they're afraid of their boss or they think their boss doesn't like them. Sometimes it's both.

The boss thing. It has become a familiar issue to me, having coached people now for many years.

For Eva, a seasoned manager in Human Resources in her early fifties, it was both. Eva believed her boss, Brian, wanted her out. Not just out of her current role. Out of the company completely.

"I'm not doing so well. I'm angry; I'm snapping at people," she said. "I don't know if I can stay in my job the way things are going."

Another time, she said, "Things with my manager aren't going well, and I don't know what to do." Or, "Brian doesn't like me. I think he wants me out."

"Have you spoken to Brian?" I'd ask.

"Absolutely not. No way."

The child in the room

At first glance, Eva did not typify someone who could be easily intimidated, but I have found that the fear of one's boss is pretty universal. More than in any other relationship, the inherent power differential can evoke authority issues—or in psychoanalytic terms—"transference," pulling us into a younger state of consciousness where we relate to our boss like they are a parent or another powerful figure from our past. Time and again, I'm confronted by people whose relationship with their boss has degenerated and become toxic.

It's not always easy to get at the truth. The thing is, no one walks into a coaching session and says, "I'm afraid of my boss." Instead, it begins with something outsized, vague, and irrational. Frequently, it's actually difficult to follow the conversation.

These initial meetings remind me of my young son waking up in the middle of the night, fearful and confused. He might say something like, "I think . . . I think there's something in my room. I heard something . . ." But he's unable to describe exactly what is scaring him.

In the same way, Eva wasn't making much sense the first time we met. She came to me with a long and successful HR career and had landed at a financial services company. Her boss had some steep expectations and personal idiosyncrasies that weren't to everyone's taste.

"He's a big picture, strategic thinker, and he doesn't have any patience for details," Eva said. She spoke quickly and loudly with emotional intensity, but I couldn't fully understand why. Nor could she.

Something about her level of fear and powerlessness seemed out of proportion.

What's going on?

The first step is to get past the vague and irrational and try to reach the heart of the problem.

As with most of these situations, there was some truth in Eva's fears. Her boss Brian wasn't happy with how she was doing at work, and that was why Eva was asked to come and see me in the first place. But Eva's fears went far beyond this. Her mind had gone into a primitive place of existential fear, where she believed she was going to lose her job and livelihood. She had jumped several steps forward, from having a problem with his work to ending up on the street.

I've discussed this earlier. If you're having a feeling, you're almost always having a thought, though you may not even be aware of it. I asked Eva to help me unpack all of this.

"Tell me what's going on," I said. "Tell me why you're feeling this way, or at least why you think you're feeling this way."

I am inspired by Brené Brown's work, among others, and pulling from her approach, I can put this another way: *What's the story you're telling yourself right now about this?* The narratives we create deeply influence how we feel about ourselves.

As we began to explore Eva's thinking, what emerged was a story that centered on Brian. *Brian thinks I'm incompetent. Brian thinks he's smarter than me. Brian wants me out.* In meetings with Brian's boss, Eva would sort of cower at Brian's side of the table and either agree stonily or become super defensive with whatever Brian said. She couldn't find a middle ground.

Eva was sufficiently self-aware, however, to know that she could also have a tendency to lose her temper if she felt threatened. If someone disagreed with her, she believed they weren't just disagreeing with her, they were trying to undermine her.

Also, while Eva had a thorough understanding of the nuts and bolts of the HR function after a decade of rising up the ranks, her organization was in the midst of a culture change initiative. She found herself faced with a new and unfamiliar approach to something called "strategic talent management" within her company. Rather than accept that she needed help to get up to speed—help that Brian was ready to give—she believed that her own expertise and experience were being devalued.

As is common in these situations, the stresses of Eva's working life also had spilled over into her home life. She had become argumentative and cranky with her wife, and she was waking at two in the morning, endlessly replaying meetings with Brian and running through all of the emotions that went with them.

As always, I was trying to explore the situation, trying to get the lay of the land, trying to bring awareness to Eva's behavior. And I was trying to be compassionate too. Sometimes it's hard for people to name that feeling, to acknowledge that what they're talking about is fear. Feeling frightened puts us in a vulnerable space. At the beginning, Eva was not in a place where she could even name it. It was all *Brian, Brian, Brian.*

I asked her, "It seems like you're frightened, Eva, is that right? Is that what you're feeling?"

As we talked, she was able to say yes, she was frightened—and angry and hurt.

"If you had to identify how old you are right now, what would you say?" I asked. "What I mean is, what emotional age do you feel you are when you experience these feelings?"

There was a long silence in the room as Eva sat staring into the middle distance.

Eventually, she said, "I don't know. Eleven, maybe? Twelve?"

"Let's talk about that time in your life. What was going on then?"

Eva had immigrated to Queens, New York, from Honduras when she was about that age. She had been eager to fit in and adapt to her new home, but she was still learning English and most of her classmates were from the Dominican Republic and Puerto Rico.

For nearly a year after she arrived, she felt frightened much of the time and intimidated by teachers, classmates, and her new American life. She felt fearful walking to school in her neighborhood, afraid that some rough kids would play a cruel joke on her. Though her parents were loving, given their own preoccupation with immigrating to the United States and finding work, they weren't very emotionally available.

"They both worked two jobs, and I had to help raise my younger sister," she said. "I kind of felt on my own much of the time. They weren't able to be there for me."

It's possible to hold two feelings at once—to be upset at our parents, for instance, and to love them. However difficult, it leads to emotional maturity and greater wisdom.

As Eva described the situation to me, I noticed that her story had a dramatic quality to it. I'm listening for this element in my client's stories, because it gives me information. When things appear stark and polarized, we are usually, unconsciously, playing one of three roles in a "drama triangle": the victim, the villain, or the hero. By definition, the drama triangle roles are simplistic and one-dimensional. This is what I often see among people who are afraid of their boss. This person has become a monolithic, scary protagonist who is responsible for their jobs and paychecks, and they're usually the victim in the story.

When a client shares that perspective, I also know I'm sitting with someone in more of a Child state of consciousness. They are not able to see their bosses as people with their own complex needs and motivations who may have positional authority but (unless they are sadistic) also likely wants them to succeed.

When we get out of the Child state and drama triangle, we can get out of our fear and mature. Everything turns to technicolor and is much more nuanced. That's a sign of a mature mind and growing up at work.

For Eva, living with fear as a child became a familiar feeling, one that she was returning to, unconsciously, in her interactions with Brian.

Up until the situation with Brian, her childhood and immigrant background felt strongly behind her. Eva ended up being a strong student in school. She was the first member of her family to attend college, and afterward, she got her first job in the HR department of a consumer products company based in New York City. She didn't know much about the field back then, but over several years, she had accumulated valuable experience in areas like benefits, compensation, and payroll. When she took the job in her current company, the financial services firm, she felt confident that she could bring all of her experience to bear in a meaningful way.

Brian, however, had new and different ideas about Human Resources. In fact, he revised his own title to be the "Director of People" instead of Director of Human Resources. Brian wanted fresh thinking and modern ways of engaging with employees, whom he treated as his "clients."

Unfortunately, all Eva could see was a threat. And so, her response was defensive. She felt that she needed to protect herself.

Parent-Adult-Child

For a few weeks, I simply got to know Eva. I found that she was a kind and gentle person, and that she was sensitive. In all of her stories, I also noted that Eva was always the *victim*, and Brian was essentially the *villain*.

After observing this pattern repeatedly, I stood up and went to my whiteboard.

"OK, I want to tell you about something, Eva."

I wrote the letters "P-A-C" on the board, standing for Parent-Adult-Child and explained to her one of the primary tenets of the Transactional Analysis model. It outlines three emotional states that characterize our consciousness and our behavior in any given moment. When we're in Child state, we're usually feeling vulnerable and scared. We think in terms of extremes: always or nevers. We are usually the *victim* of life and of others' actions. When we're feeling threatened and we're in Child state, we tend to engage in one of three basic survival mechanisms: fight, flight, or freeze. We might scream or yell. We can lose control out of fear.

Now, there is an upside to this state, to all of these states. The Child state comes with imagination, it comes with playfulness, it comes with creativity, but the child should not really be running the show on any regular basis in an adult's life. A child has limited options to deal with a threat or difficult experience. A child has tantrums when they're upset. Their feelings are bigger than their body can tolerate. A child does not make a good manager. A child sees herself as smaller, less important, and less powerful than others.

Then there's the "Parent state." On the face of it, this sounds good, but when you're in the Parent state, you've got to make sure other people do what they're supposed to do; you need to be in control. There's an authoritarian quality to it. Sometimes it's needed: *We are leaving the house in five minutes, so you've got to have your shoes on.*

The Parent state implies a dynamic where you have more power than the other person. Sometimes that's appropriate but it ought to be used sparingly.

Finally, we have our "Adult state." This is the state we really want to be in most of the time, especially at work. If I'm showing up as the fully fledged adult, that means that I'm going to take responsibility for my feelings and my reactions and my relationships with others. I recognize my agency and its limitations. I'm not going to regress into Child state (or if I do, I'll note it and try to shift out of it). I'm not going to do a power play and try to be your parent. I am also going to treat you as the adult you are. We're going to treat each other as equals. Adult state is our most healthy form of being and our most mature source of managing and leading others.

When I asked Eva which state she thought she was in when dealing with Brian, she was unequivocal in her answer.

"Child state. Definitely Child state."

Sometimes in a session, you can see the *aha* moments as they're happening; you can see these beautiful insights dawn. This is how it was with Eva. I then asked the question I usually ask at this point.

"So, how's this working for you, Eva?"

She shook her head. "Not good. Not good at all."

Reconnecting the parts

I wanted Eva to feel fully what it was like to be in the Child state—to make the unconscious conscious—so I asked her first to sit and invoke that state—to notice, feel, and accept the fear that went with it. I then asked her to switch chairs, invoke her Adult state, and look across the room at the empty chair, where her inner child sat.

This exercise requires a little imagination. I'm asking the client to embody an unconscious dynamic they've never brought to life before.

"What do you notice when you look at younger Eva?"

"She's small," Eva replied. "She looks small to me. She also looks vulnerable. I want to take care of her; I want to protect her."

"OK. You want to tell her that?"

Now, instead of just talking *about* young Eva, I'm trying to make the work dialogic. I'm trying to create a connection between the different parts of Eva—parts that were divided or in conflict. We can so often cut off and reject some part of ourselves because it's too painful to tolerate. Often, that is where our spiritual and emotional pain begins.

What our inner child needs to know is that we're protected, that we're safe. They need to know that they don't have to run the show; they don't have to be overwhelmed.

I said to the adult Eva, "OK, you see how the child Eva has been acting with Brian. She's scared of him and sometimes he loses his temper out of frustration. What would it be like if there were more of *you* in the room? What could *you* do to support little Eva?"

Eva sat a little straighter and said, "I would tell little Eva, 'You don't have to be afraid. Brian is a person. Brian is our new manager. He has different ideas than we do, but he's not going to hurt you. You're OK and I'm going to make sure you're OK. I'm here and I'm not going anywhere.'"

Be the adult in the room

I've worked with enough executives by now to see a pattern: A lot of very successful people fear one day they are going wind up homeless with nothing and living under a bridge. It's classic scarcity mindset. That leads me to help them test that set of assumptions because nine times out of ten, it's based on a model of catastrophe versus reality. It's a cognitive distortion that makes them think, if I lose this job, I'll never get another one, I'll lose all my money, I'll become homeless, and so on. But none of that has actually happened or is likely to happen. It's a *projection* of their fear. (To be sure, there are managers who do wish to fire their employees, and this is a real fear that may require attention. More often than not, though, the existential fear I hear has more to do with the client's transference than the reality at hand.)

It's important for us to name the fear, which assumes we will have no support and few resources. Once we start envisioning worst-case scenarios, it may be initially terrifying but there's also something strangely liberating about it. It allows us to shift into problem-solving mode.

I asked Eva, "What's the worst that could happen here?"

"Well, I guess at some point Brian just won't want me in this job," Eva said. "I'll get fired."

Her face looked calmer as she envisioned this scenario.

"OK, and then what would you do?" I asked.

"Well, it's not easy for a fifty-three-year-old to find work, but I guess I'd look for another job."

"Do you know how you would do that?"

"I might call some of the people I've worked with in the past, my network," she said. "Update my LinkedIn profile. Things like that."

"Makes sense."

She continued, "I might look into that company near my home that I've wondered about. I'd have such a short commute."

"Sounds good," I said. "And you and your wife have your house paid off, don't you?"

She nodded.

"And your wife has a good job?"

"Yes, she does."

Eva was beginning to see her fears as less like scary shadows on the wall as she approached the situation from a mature and resolute Adult perspective and got into problem-solving mode. The fact was, she worked in HR, so she knew how people found jobs, and her mind's executive function began kicking in. The opposite of victim consciousness is creator consciousness, when we ask ourselves what we want and what we *could* want.

"So, it's fair to say you'd be OK, that you'd figure something out?" I asked her. "You've done that before."

"Yeah, sure, I'd figure it out," she said. "I might not even want to stay in this job anyway, because I don't really like working for Brian so much."

All of a sudden, we're not the victim anymore. We're not this little creature who's at the mercy of circumstances and lives by someone else's rules. We're grown-ups, making grown-up choices.

My invitation to Eva was to be *the adult in the room*. Though a multilayered statement, it starts with us being aware of which state we are in. We have no chance of changing anything in ourselves until we know from what place we are starting. From there, the idea is that no matter what state you're in, the hope is that you can shift into your Adult state as quickly as possible. The part of you that can stay calm, listen, be influenced, and see other sides to a story. The part that isn't reactive, defensive, or aggressive, but balanced and whole.

In this sense, the Transactional Analysis model—specifically identifying the Parent, Adult, and Child within us—can sometimes feel a little like a magic trick. I had another client recently, a man in his twenties, who couldn't talk about his boss without going pale and looking frightened. I wrote those three words on my white board, and as I explained what it was all about, I could see again the sudden insight; he felt the truth of the model almost instantly.

Fritz Perls believed that awareness is curative. Once you realize what's going on inside of you and how you're showing up, the light bulb goes on. The insight alone can cause a change in how you experience your situation.

The "after" picture

When we think of leadership, we tend to think of leading others. I think it's worthwhile to borrow author Stephen Covey's idea that leadership actually begins with leading yourself. Can you lead others well if you're leading yourself badly? I've known leaders who pound their fists on tables when they're angry. Others scare employees with mean-spirited criticism or eye-rolling impatience. These sorts of behaviors are indicators that we're in Child (or Parent) state—not the source of mature leadership.

By bringing awareness to our behavior, we can identify which state we're in and guide ourselves toward where we need to be. The Child state may allow you to express your creativity and playfulness, but it isn't appropriate in most workplace situations. While the Parent state may sometimes be necessary, it implies an unequal power dynamic and so has only limited applications.

Leaders must be intentional about leading as often as possible from an Adult state. This is important for many reasons. First, whether we realize it or not, we transmit our emotional state to everyone around us. When Eva was in Child state, scared and petulant, it's likely that Brian unconsciously showed up in Parent state, admonishing and authoritarian.

Being in a Child state also means we're likely in the aforementioned drama triangle, unconsciously playing the victim to the Parent villain. (By the way, we're big fans of the Conscious Leadership Group, which suggests that if we're in the drama triangle, we actually can't express mature, conscious leadership.)

By invoking her Adult state, Eva could begin to articulate what it meant to lead herself at work *in concert* with her inner child. She had to counsel and support her inner child. *I am sorry you're so afraid, but I'm going to protect you. You don't have to do this alone.*

I worked with Eva for about six months, and during the latter half of that period, I witnessed a subtle but profound change in her. The person coming to see me was no longer the Child. She had become much more measured, much more mature. The vagueness and uncertainty had melted away. She was no longer living in extremes.

She could say, "Things are better this week with Brian," or "This week wasn't so good with him." She was no longer terrorized. There were no more extreme worst-case scenarios or I'm-hiding-under-the-desk feelings.

The beauty of the Adult state is that when we are whole, we are more creative and resourceful. When a problem arises, we simply consider our options and figure out what we're going to do. What's more, we're far more present in the moment. When we lead from our Adult state, we can set a productive tone and inspire those vital qualities in others, in a meeting or companywide. The stakes are high. We are all better in the workplace when we function as Adults.

When Eva was in Child state, she either felt triggered in a past state of fear or she projected six months ahead of herself, fired and living on the streets. Now, instead of collapsing or retreating or being defensive, she could simply disagree with Brian and explore other options.

With intentionality, Eva could relate to Brian not as a threat but as a colleague and even as a mentor.

I no longer saw the fear in her eyes when she spoke about her boss.

"Actually, I have a lot to learn from him," Eva said. "If I'm not so busy being scared of him, he could be a great mentor to me."

Feedback from both Brian and her peers confirmed the change. Eva sometimes still got testy about things she didn't like, but she wasn't so extreme. She was more willing to listen, more open to trying new things and to accepting help. My sense was that she was choosing her battles a little more carefully. She became more relaxed.

We all grow up in many ways, but the truth is, we may always have an inner child within our psyche who feels emotionally younger than our chronological age reflects. That is perfectly OK—sweet and import- ant for healing, actually—but we have to stay aware of what's happening inside of us first.

When I touched base with Eva months later, she was working remotely as a result of the pandemic, and she was grateful for our work together.

"What are you noticing?" I asked. "What's this like, showing up differently?"

"I notice I have more of a choice about how I'll show up," she said. "I don't have to be like a child, anxious and scared. I'm also feeling less tired and stressed."

With greater energy, she had more emotional bandwidth to think about what she could learn on the job, and she was enjoying managing her own team. In a way, a younger part of Eva needed Adult Eva's attention. She just didn't need to throw a tantrum to get it.

► **REFLECTIONS** ◄

- When I'm upset in some way at work (or in life), am I in Parent, Adult, or Child state? How do I know?

- If I'm in Child state, what vulnerable situation from my child-hood does this remind me of? Did I have the support I needed as a child to manage difficult emotions? Might there be some unmet needs in terms of what I, as a child, needed but didn't get from my upbringing?

- If I'm having a difficult feeling, what am I thinking? What's the story I'm telling myself about this moment, this situation, this relationship, or this person? How do I feel when I think about this?

- Do I have a habit of experiencing life or work from a place of being the victim (or the villain or the hero)?

► **PRACTICES** ◄

- If you notice yourself drawn into Child state, take a moment to become aware of it, breathe, and try to pivot into what your inner adult would do or say.

- If necessary, take a walk or ask for a moment to collect yourself. Your inner child should not be running a meeting, having a difficult conversation, or trying to lead a team.

- As a professional and as a leader, practice communicating, managing, and leading from the psychic space of your Adult state. If you don't know what that means, ask yourself: *What does the wisest, most mature part of myself feel and think right now?*

▶ **EXPERIMENTS** ◀

- With the assistance of a therapist, coach, or trusted friend, explore the different voices inside of you, particularly your inner child. Allow yourself to embody the part of you that is unconscious and unaware.

- Play with the empty chair exercise as a way to create a conversation between your inner child and your inner adult. See what support and resources your inner adult can offer to your inner child. You can also do this in journal form.

- Experiment with spending time with your inner child. Ask what they might most like to do and do it. (This can include going to the zoo, getting an ice cream, or dancing to loud music!) Stay connected with the part of you that might need some attention and love—and consider this a lifelong exercise that never ends.

Conclusion

IN WRITING THIS BOOK, WE'VE had our own parallel experience of growing up at work. We had the original idea nearly a decade ago, but it took several years of coaching and a lot of conversations to hone our purpose and central ideas.

We had to ask ourselves why we wanted to undertake this project: *Why did we want to write a book? What did success actually mean to us?* We concluded we had something to share, and not because we wanted to build a platform. We wanted to find our own voices in an unconventional and authentic way.

As you know by now, finding your voice and defining success for yourself are critical steps in becoming more psychologically mature. If we wish to live a purposeful, reflected life, then we must look beyond the expectations transmitted through our societal conditioning. We must consider what we've been taught about success from others, and we then must find out what's true for us, now.

What emerged as true for us from our discussions is one of the messages at the heart of our book: Professional growth and personal growth are deeply intertwined. For us, success has meant being able to illustrate and expand on that concept more deeply for others.

We've tried to consolidate what we've learned over many years, connecting theory to practice. By relating our insights to the slightly esoteric field of Gestalt therapy and drawing upon the highly useful Adult Development Theory body of work, we have tried to provide context for case studies in ways that are instructive and beneficial but also practical for readers, especially if you are an emerging or senior leader.

We hope this book has been helpful to you in your own journey of growing up at work, and if you find it helpful, we encourage you to share the book with others so that you might learn together.

These case studies represent the specific, real life experiences of our clients, but we believe they also touch on issues that are deeply universal. These are human stories. They are intimate tales of emotional honesty, humility, and insights born out of self-examination, coaching support, and the commitment to growth and learning.

Across the stories, a final theme exists that we wish to share with you: the importance of having a committed, lifelong growth mindset. With a growth mindset, we approach life—our successes, failures, conflicts, and interactions—as opportunities for our learning and development. This is especially important for leaders, given their outsized effect on people and organizations, but it's true for anyone who wants to mature through work.

As far as we are concerned, none of us is ever done growing up or becoming who we are. Even now, we continue to grow up at work, and we go on a journey of learning and introspection every time we work with our clients.

We see learning as a lifelong quest, one that comes with its own value and rewards. We invite you to consider your life and your work as rich laboratories for reaching your potential. In other words, we encourage you to keep growing up at work.

Finally, we are deeply grateful to all of our clients. By working with them, we have grown as coaches, and we have grown as human beings. We hope we never stop growing up. We wish the same for you too.

—Yael and Yosh

Acknowledgments

SEVERAL YEARS AGO, AS WE found ourselves feeling stuck writing this book, Yael reached out to a Gestalt therapist named Joseph Melnick. In their conversation, Joe shared something that was tremendously helpful. He said that the experience of stuckness, according to Gestalt theory, pointed to the need for more external support. Suddenly, our stuckness was framed not as a failure of our skill or stamina, but as something that required one of the most essential aspects of a full life: more support. In a multitude of ways, we wish to thank all of those in our lives who have provided us with the helpful, generative, and loving support to bring this book to life. (And thanks to Joe for this important advice.)

We have enduring gratitude to the Esalen Institute in Big Sur, California, the auspicious setting of our first meeting and one of the central spaces in this country where Gestalt therapy was deepened, developed, and practiced. For Yael, postgraduate studies at the Gestalt Associates for Psychotherapy (GAP) in New York City supported the development of her knowledge and skills to be a Gestalt therapist and coach. Thanks to the GAP faculty, with special appreciation for her fantastic therapist and mentor, Johanna Barrett, who also reviewed this book for theoretical accuracy and endorsed it with love; to Jim Mulry, whose early Gestalt supervision was fundamental to Yael becoming a skilled therapist and coach; and to Connie Newman, for her impassioned introduction in year one to creative adjustments and interruptions in contact. Also, special thanks to Arleen Maiorano for her GAP leadership and creating a meaningful Gestalt community dedicated to learning and growth. Yael also has tremendous gratitude for having met a dear community of friends and colleagues made over years of study and practice at the GAP, including members of her GAP class and later suitemates: Sharyn Levine, Michelle Mullins, and Michael Mitchell. Yosh wishes to thank the Hakomi Institute in Germany, where he was trained, and the late Ron Kurtz for his instrumental work and soulful role-modeling of loving presence. We are both deeply grateful to Allan Whiteman, teacher, therapist, mentor. It's Allan whom we quote with the words we try to live by: "True authenticity is always a surprise." Thanks to our deepest spiritual teachers Adyashanti, Eckhart Tolle, and A.H. Almaas.

Our consulting careers began together with the support of Margaret Regan and Bill Prensky, and we thank them, as well as our FutureWork Institute (FWI) colleagues, for a decade of training, community, and exposure to consulting in organizations across the world. The foundation of working at FWI gave us the confidence and know-how to begin Collaborative Coaching nearly eleven years ago.

We also wish to thank the many organizational clients who have worked with Collaborative Coaching over the years (you know who you are!). We are grateful for your courage and trust to partner with us, and to work with depth, honesty, and vulnerability in our collaboration together. Thank you for accepting our idea that personal and professional growth are deeply interconnected, and that emotional maturity makes for better leadership and teams.

For early support and endorsements of our book, we wholeheartedly thank Bob Kaplan, Marshall Goldsmith, Lisa Laskow Lahey, Kef Kasdin, Sarah Larson Levey, Johanna Barrett, Kerry Docherty, Laura O'Loughlin, Robert Bank, and Joseph Melnick.

There are many individual coaching clients whom we also wish to thank here, but out of respect for their privacy, we do so without naming them. Special thanks to the coaching clients who reviewed and approved their stories for publication in this book. Yael also wishes to give a personal shout-out to the nearly 150 leaders she has taught in the Emerging Leaders program of Princeton AlumniCorps over the past nine years. Working with all of you helped Yael deeply understand leadership development as an inside-out process. Your vulnerable, authentic, real-life stories are woven through this book in many ways.

We wish to thank our family, friends, and community for their love and support. Starting with special thanks to our families—Isak and Marti Sivi, Rachel Sivi, Mark Ravreby, Phyllis Ravreby, Christa and Karl-Heinz Beier, and Marcus Beier—who supported us to believe in ourselves and who gave us the confidence to cultivate lives of meaning and inspiration. Our special gratitude to Marti, in conjunction with cousins Andy and Coleen Ravreby, for being early readers of this book and for your helpful feedback.

Special thanks to dear friends of many years who have supported us along the journeys of our life, including Anna and Thomas Riquier (shout-out to Anna for reminding me about "take back your eyes" and for three decades of honest and loving friendship), Thomas Weidman and Claudia Kühne, Susannah Kirsch, Abbe Wertz, Heather Frank, Laura O'Loughlin and Greg Snyder, Elizabeth Puccini and Loren Runnels, Malancha Chanda, Emily Rosen, and Ramon Marmolejos. Another wholehearted thank you goes from Yosh to Gudrun Saydan-König, who not only offered Yosh his first "real" job, but also a friendship and a professional partnership that resulted in the joint discovery of Hakomi.

Thanks to our supportive community in Maplewood, including Sarah and Doug Cox, the Dowds (special thanks to Kathy for the title help and Mark for hiking support), Claire Kaplan and Stephanie Bourgeois for our heartful Monday morning walks in the reservation, and Andrew Boyarsky and Jim Lear for meaningful times by the fire; Teal and Nat Paynter, the Wissel-Hastings, the Davenports, and the Vitale clan.

Early and late support for the writing and editing of this book was critical to its momentum and completion. We are also humbled at how many people it takes to make a book come to life. Our thanks to Nancy Erickson, John Hearne, and Jonathan Gifford for outlining, coaching, interviewing, and early drafting support. Our gratitude also to the Greenleaf Book Group publishing team including Jen Glynn, Erin Brown, Pamela Ferdinand, Judy Marchman, Mimi Bark, David Endris, Corrin Foster, Tiffany Barrientos, and others for helping us "land the plane." We have felt very supported by your team; thank you for ensuring that our book stayed true to our voice and our values.

Being co-parents, life partners, and business owners is an intense and deeply meaningful experience. Yael and Yosh thank each other for the love, patience, humor, and inspiration, and for a conversation that started in 2003 and has continued ever since.

Finally, special thanks to our little guy, Noah. We have always been a tight little family, but through COVID-19 quarantine, we became even tighter. We hope that this book helps you to better understand what we do for a living. (And Mama is sorry for missing some soccer games to get it done.) Noah, we love the person you are, and we are honored to be your parents.

About the Authors

YAEL C. SIVI, LCSW

The lead author of *Growing Up at Work*, Yael is an executive coach and a Gestalt psychotherapist. Her expertise is helping people grow psychologically so they can lead with greater integrity and relate more authentically to others.

Yael's work takes place at the intersection of professional growth and personal transformation. With an academic background in urban studies from Macalester College, a Master of Science in industrial social work from Columbia University, a postgraduate fellowship in Gestalt psychology from the Gestalt Associates for Psychotherapy in New York City, and a career of nearly twenty years as an executive coach, psychotherapist, and organizational consultant, Yael lends her expertise to helping people grow, lead, and collaborate with emotional maturity.

While Yael originally set out to be a psychotherapist, her trajectory changed early in her career when she realized that the complex dynamics that exist within families and individuals also exist in organizations. She observed that the human dynamics at the workplace hold great potential for individual and group transformation.

For two decades, Yael has worked with thousands of employees, managers, and leaders in Fortune 1000 companies and nonprofit organizations on topics related to authentic leadership, emotional intelligence, and conscious collaboration.

In *Growing Up at Work,* Yael draws on coaching and psychotherapy to bring adult development, Gestalt, and other theories to life: our work life. By presenting real-life case studies, she examines how work-related dilemmas for professionals often lead to an equally personal journey of growth and evolution.

YOSH C. BEIER, MSC

Trained as a scientist, consultant, mediator, and therapist, Yosh brings a highly interdisciplinary background to his role of executive coach and consultant. Combining analytical skills, systemic thinking, and a deep understanding of human behavior, Yosh speaks both the language of human and organizational dynamics.

A native of Germany who moved to New York, he has worked as an executive and leadership coach for nearly two decades—and brings his experience as a global organizational effectiveness consultant and high-performance team coach to his engagements.

Shifting from an academic career in theoretical physics to consulting, Yosh quickly realized that the main reasons projects succeeded or failed nearly always lay beyond matters of technical expertise or project management and had all to do with human dynamics. Intrigued and driven by a desire to better understand how to facilitate and support individual and interpersonal growth, Yosh trained first to become a therapist and subsequently a mediator, executive coach, and Scrum Master.

Yosh has worked with many Fortune 1000 companies and various nonprofit, governmental, and nongovernmental organizations. He is a managing partner and cofounder of Collaborative Coaching. Yosh has served as the board chair of a Buddhist nonprofit organization, as well as heading its strategic planning committee, among other roles.

Yosh serves as coauthor with Yael of *Growing Up at Work*. The book represents years of their work together translating concepts from the world of psychotherapy and coaching into the workplace for more authentic and effective leadership and team collaboration.

> > > < < <

LEARN MORE ABOUT THE LIFELONG PRACTICES AT THE HEART OF GROWING UP AT WORK. TAKE OUR E-CLASS AT:

growingupatwork.com

FOR MORE INFORMATION ABOUT OUR FIRM OR TO CONTACT US, PLEASE VISIT:

Collaborative-Coaching.com